Firestarters

100 Job Profiles to Inspire Young Women

KELLY BEATTY

DALE SALVAGGIO BRADSHAW

Firestarters

© 2006 by Kelly Beatty and Dale Salvaggio Bradshaw

Acquisitions and Development Editor: Lori Cates Hand
Interior Designer: Nick Anderson
Cover Designer: Trudy Coler
Page Layout Coordinators: Carolyn Newland, Trudy Coler
Proofreader: Paula Lowell
Indexer: Tina Trettin

Printed in the United States of America

11 10 09 08 07 06   9 8 7 6 5 4 3 2 1

Library of Congress Cataloging-in-Publication Data

Beatty, Kelly, 1969-
    Firestarters : 100 job profiles to inspire young women / Kelly Beatty and Dale Salvaggio Bradshaw.
        p. cm.
    Includes index.
    ISBN 1-59357-310-3 (alk. paper)
1. Vocational guidance for women . 2. Work--Psychological aspects.
    I. Bradshaw, Dale Salvaggio, 1970- II. Title.
    HF5382.6.B43 2006
    331.702082--dc22
                                2005036852

ISBN-10 1-59357-310-3
ISBN-13 978-1-59357-310-2

About This Book

✳ This book is a helpful reference for high school and college women that describes 100 interesting professions in an informative and positive format. With a fun and personal approach, *Firestarters* demonstrates the power of networking and the limitless career opportunities available to young women today. It also gives invaluable advice from real women and inspires and motivates readers to think about and explore career possibilities.

The interviews of 100 real women are presented in easy-to-read, succinct profiles that outline a job description, day-to-day responsibilities, the woman's job likes and challenges, her education and work experiences, and professional and personal advice she has to offer young women in choosing a career. The profiles provide a glimpse into each woman's job, and will help readers determine which careers might fit their personalities and talents.

We wanted to write this book because as women in our mid-thirties, we realize how important it is to find a personally satisfying career. A lack of knowledge makes it difficult to do this. We both started thinking, "Wouldn't it be great if there were a book that showcased the wide range of careers that women now hold? Something like that could really help young women narrow their focus and not feel clueless about choosing a career." We wished we had something like this book to turn to when we were in high school and college. We've both had ups and downs in searching for a job that gives us meaning, and although it's not impossible to go back and learn a new career at our age, it's more difficult than if we were in our late teens/early twenties. That's why it's so important for young women to find what they are passionate about, to learn what they like and dislike, and to really search for a career that will be fulfilling to them. This book is just the tip of an enormous iceberg waiting to be melted by future Firestarters.

Acknowledgments

Writing *Firestarters* has been a wonderful experience for us not only because it is a project we felt passionate about, but it also fulfills us to know that we are giving back just a little. Our goal was to help enrich the lives of young women, but our lives have been enriched in the process. We feel an immense amount of gratitude to a great many people.

This book would not have been possible without the 102 women who took time out of their busy lives to tell their stories. To our mothers, sisters, aunts, friends, friends of friends, and "Carolina" girls, thank you. You were so giving of your time, and we learned so much from each of you. Bruce Gamble, your willingness to look at our query letters and writing helped us refine our work. Nan Graham, your own publishing stories helped us navigate the publishing waters. Thank you Tom Douglass for helping us form our corporate identity, Indigo Rose. Lori Cates Hand, you're one heck of an editor. Thank you for making us dig deeper.

—Kelly and Dale

I am grateful to many people, and to try and list them all here could backfire. I'm sure that I'll forget someone. Dale, you're first on the list. We have had so many hare-brained, crazy ideas, and we finally followed our own advice to be fearless and take risks. To my "grils" in Raleigh, thanks for not laughing when I told you I was writing a book. I cannot neglect to mention my husband's eagle eyes and attention to detail. You saved us from a few catastrophes. Lastly, I want to thank my parents. I can remember you telling me that I could be anything I wanted when I grew up. I've never forgotten that, and I'm still working on it.

—Kelly

To my husband Steve, thank you for never laughing at my dreams; for your constant support, humor, and love; and for all the nights you put the kids to bed while I worked. Thank you to my parents for giving me a solid foundation and confidence that has enabled me to create and accomplish goals. And to my children, Charlie and Sophia, thank you for enriching my life every day. And I've saved the best for last, Kelly. We've taken our friendship to new levels. What a roller-coaster of experiences we've had writing this book together. I am so glad that I was in the seat with you.

—Dale

Firestarters

(fīr'start'-erz)

women blazing their own trails to fulfilling careers that

complement the lives they want to lead.

Dedications

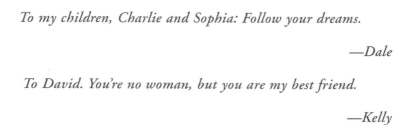

To my children, Charlie and Sophia: Follow your dreams.

—Dale

To David. You're no woman, but you are my best friend.

—Kelly

Contents

Contents

Introduction

Former First Lady Hillary Clinton tells a story in her biography (*Living History*, Scribner, 2004) of wanting to be an astronaut as an early teen. It was the beginning of the Space Age, and she wrote to NASA offering to volunteer for astronaut training. Imagine her disappointment when she received a letter informing her that NASA wasn't accepting women into its program. That's hard to imagine. She isn't much older than your mother, but she grew up in a time when women didn't have the choices that you now have. You are so lucky to be a young woman at the dawn of a new millennium, and you'll see just how lucky as you read about some of the many career possibilities available to you.

Choosing your own career is a difficult decision. Where do you even start? That's where this book can help. Use it as a springboard for exploration, and think of the profiles as mini career days. It's our hope that you will achieve your destiny more directly if you look at your opportunities now. We think your career should be personally fulfilling, in addition to just paying the bills.

Each of the women in *Firestarters* has a career that she worked very hard to achieve. You'll see that it doesn't matter where you grew up or how much money your parents make. You have what it takes to be whatever you want. Some of these women make a lot of money and some don't, but we don't think that money is the definition of success. Success is finding happiness in what you do.

Having a job that you don't like can feel like sitting through your least favorite class—not for one hour, but for eight, everyday. That's why it's really important that you alone decide what kind of career you want. Your individual interests make you unique and special. You can combine those interests, talents, and strengths to find a career that's right for you.

Not only are you in charge of finding the most fitting career for yourself, but you also have control over how your career affects your desired lifestyle. Want to work from home or maybe travel for a living? Modern technology and an increase in job flexibility all make it possible. And, don't think that once your mind is made up that you can't change it. You'll meet lots of women who did the same thing for years before deciding that they needed a change. They figured out that if they were going to do something everyday, they had better love it. You'll also meet women who have taken time out of their careers to raise their children and women who have found a balance between work and family.

We can't wait for you to read this book because we had a lot of fun writing it. What's really amazing is that the women interviewed are just a small sampling of career possibilities. These are just women that the two of us know personally or through various contacts. It would be impossible for us to include every potential job. Isn't that exciting to know that you have more opportunities than we could ever write about?

Read on to "spark" your imagination.

> **Note:** As would be expected, some of our interviewees' jobs and job responsibilities might have changed since the time of their interview.

"Inside every block of stone there dwells a masterpiece; all one

must do is remove the excess stone to reveal a gift."

—Michelangelo

Job Profiles

Alisa Salvaggio

Natural Light Photographer

{ *"I like to capture their personality, who they are... not just the person, but their personality, too."* }

Job Description

Alisa prefers the outdoors as her photography studio, where she uses daylight for her lighting and natural settings for her backgrounds. The majority of her work is photographing children, families, and special events (weddings and community functions). Alisa also enjoys still-life photography and sells these photos locally.

A Day on the Job

Prepares for the photo shoot by planning the order of the photos to be taken and making a reminder list of requested poses. If Alisa is not familiar with the photography site, she visits it prior to the shoot and notes good shot locations. • Gathers equipment and makes sure it is working properly—"I don't want to forget anything; extra batteries, film, all that stuff." • Photographs her client(s). Each shoot usually takes from 30 minutes to an hour. Special events, such as weddings, require longer hours. • Takes film to and from the developer. • Packages proofs in a creative and organized presentation for the client. • Reviews the proofs with her client. • Orders requested prints. • Markets her business through mailings and by displaying her work at local restaurants and businesses.

3

Job Likes

"I like to capture their personality, who they are… not just the person, but their personality, too." • "It fits into my life. I like the convenience of being able to set my own hours." Alisa is a stay-at-home mom and the hours fit her schedule well. • Alisa finds the pay good for what she feels is a short amount of time to work. • "Being with the kids and the families, it's just fun. It doesn't even seem like a job. I guess because I love it so much."

Job Challenges

"The weather. The other day I had a photo shoot and it started to rain." Other than that, Alisa can't think of any other dislikes.

Steps to Current Job

- Southern University in Chattanooga, Tennessee, nursing and music courses.
- Blue Ridge Community College in Hendersonville, North Carolina, Associate Degree in Nursing (ADN).
- Stay-at-home mom and part-time nurse for a pediatric office for two years; took photography classes at Blue Ridge Community College.
- Stay-at-home mom and part-time photographer.

Advice

As Alisa develops her own photography business, she realizes that the more education you have in photography, the more credible, knowledgeable, and confident you'll be as a photographer. She also says, "In this type of profession, you have to keep up with technology." Alisa is currently working on a Web site where her photos will be posted for her clients to review. "Clients demand the 'latest thing.' I have to continue to upgrade."

"Do what you love. Do what you are good at. Do what you are passionate about. It doesn't matter how much money it makes."

Helpful Personality Traits

Creative, comfortable taking charge of a situation, good communicator, and a people person.

Hobbies & Interests

Running, photography, piano, and reading.

Alyson Rhodes-Murphy

Assistant Museum Curator

{ *"I love working with historical objects—looking at them, handling them, and listening to the stories they tell me."* }

Job Description
"I'm basically the guardian of the museum objects." Alyson is an Assistant Curator, and as such, she works as the Collection Manager and Registrar of historical resources for a local government agency. Alyson is responsible for the physical care and documentation of the museum objects.

A Day on the Job
Monitors museum exhibit and storage spaces by checking for correct temperature, humidity, and appropriate security, and makes sure no pests are in the environment. • Cares for the museum collection by cleaning, checking the condition, and ensuring the proper storage of objects. • Documents and maintains collection records; this includes recording the history of an object, doing the legal paperwork involved with purchasing objects, buying insurance, conducting appraisals, performing inventories, completing gift and loan forms, keeping exhibit ledgers, and following proper accession and documentation procedures to add objects to the permanent museum collection. • "I also conduct research, install exhibits, work during special events and living history programs, and give lectures." Alyson explains, "Every museum is different, depending on size, budget, staff, private, public, etc. Museum staff generally wear lots of hats, and it's rare that you find a position in which you have only one role."

Job Likes
"I love working with historical objects—looking at them, handling them, and listening to the stories they tell me." • "It's very rewarding to know that I'm helping to save a piece of history. I feel like I'm doing something worthwhile, something that makes a difference." • "I look forward to going to work everyday."

Job Challenges
"Lots of paperwork." Museums are required to document everything, and the paperwork can be tedious and time-consuming.

Steps to Current Job

- University of North Carolina at Greensboro, Bachelor of Science in Textiles Product Marketing; joined Costume Society of America and volunteered at the local historical society.
- Worked in sales promotions for a large department store for five years doing visual merchandising, special events, and fashion merchandising.
- Iowa State in Ames, Master's degree in Textiles with emphasis in History and Conservation; volunteered and interned with local history museums, held an *assistantship* as Collection Manager for the school's costume collection, and joined the American Association of Museums (AAM) and the American Association of State and Local History (AASLH).
- Assistant Museum Curator with Historic Preservation and Museum Services for a division of the local Recreation and Parks department.

Advice

Alyson suggests getting a degree in art history, history, or museum studies. It is also helpful to know that a lot of museums prefer advanced degrees. "Museum jobs are tough to come by, so get as much museum experience as you can as a volunteer. Internships and volunteer work are essential! Many of my job duties require skills I learned through volunteer work, not in the classroom." She also advises joining professional museum organizations. "These organizations have newsletters, Web sites, conferences, and professional training workshops to keep you up-to-date and to help you meet others in the field."

"It's easier said than done, but money really isn't all that important. Yes, you have to have enough to live off of, but choose a career that will make you happy, one that will make you excited to go to work, one that is emotionally and mentally rewarding. It makes such a difference in your professional *and* personal life."

Helpful Personality Traits

Inquisitive, enjoys investigating and the "quest" for information, independent, a good writer, able to view history objectively, organized, detail-oriented, and patient.

Hobbies & Interests

Taking care of her young son, travel, visiting museum exhibits, going to clubs for live music, reading fantasy fiction, bird watching, walking in the woods, and relaxing with her husband. Her main interests are historical costume and textiles, and she is also interested in women's history, social history, and domestic science history.

> An **assistantship** is a job that a student gets through a university. The money earned from an assistantship is a form of financial aid.

Ami Vitale

Independent Photojournalist

{ *"I am one lucky cat who gets paid to do what she loves."* }

Job Description
Ami works all over the world telling journalistic or newsworthy stories, primarily through the use of pictures.

A Day on the Job
Depending on the assignment, Ami might follow nomads through mountains or look for elephants in the remote corners of India. • Works with local people in foreign countries and sometimes their governments to get permission to visit remote areas. • Applies for *grants* (filling out applications, writing proposals) to fund her projects. • Organizes photographs in a way that tells a story. • Writes text that complements her photographs. • Finds publications to buy her stories and photos.

Job Likes
Ami loves the freedom and "the privilege of seeing so many extraordinary places and meeting amazing people from all walks of life."

Job Challenges
Because she is often in war-torn areas of the world, Ami says it's hard "witnessing the terrible things man does to one another because of fear and ignorance, but there is always joy in the saddest places, and my worst day is still a privilege."

Steps to Current Job
- University of North Carolina at Chapel Hill, Bachelor of Arts in International Studies.
- Editor, Associated Press, for four years.
- Photographer/Editor for one year.
- Independent Photojournalist. Since going out on her own, Ami has won numerous awards and received several grants, such as World Press Photos, for photos taken in 2004 and 2002; Magazine Photographer of the Year,

2003, National Press Photographers Association; First Place for the 2002 Society of American Travel Writers Foundation; PDN's 2002 Best Website; Canon Female Photojournalist Grant, 2003, awarded at Perpignan by the French Association of Women Journalists (AFJ) and Canon Communication. For a complete listing, visit Ami's Web site at www.amivitale.com.

Advice
Ami explains that in her field, experience, risk taking, and exploration are more valuable than a formal education. She also thinks, "It's important not to focus on the things that hold you back; but to know there is always another path to get where you want to be."

Helpful Personality Traits
A love of meeting people and adventurous. Ami says, "If you need a lot of stability and do not like spontaneity, this is not a good job."

Hobbies & Interests
Horseback riding, skiing, mountain biking, trekking, and hanging out on sunny days with family and friends.

> A *grant* is a giving of funds, either private or public, for a specific purpose that is considered valuable or helpful by the organization that gives the grant.

Andrea Lekberg

Pastry Chef/Artist*

{ *"I like making things. I like the detail of it. Right now I get to think about gingerbread houses."* }

Job Description
"I work at a place that's more of a bakery. So we make things for people to take home." As the pastry chef for a small patisserie, Andrea oversees the daily production of pastries, pastry displays, wedding and special-occasion cakes; and the ordering of supplies and ingredients.

On a rooftop in Brooklyn, pastry chef Andrea Lekburg completes a wedding cake just in time for the party.

A Day on the Job

Gets to the bakery around 4 a.m. • Notes what is left over from the day before: "I look at what is left over to see what I have to make that day." • Makes breakfast pastries. • Fills the display cases with items that were prepped the day before, "putting out cakes or pastries for that day." • Starts production for the next day. "We're always a day ahead." • Orders needed supplies and ingredients. • Makes wedding and special-occasion cakes between the preceding tasks. Wedding cakes involve consultations with the clients, tasting, baking, and decorating.

Job Likes

"I love the work. I love waking up in the morning, going to the shop, making coffee." • "I like making things. I like the detail of it. Right now I get to think about gingerbread houses." • "I like the physical work, which is something you absolutely have to like if you are going to get into pastry. You are on your feet all day, and sometimes you're picking up bags of flour, you're kneading things, and using your hands for detail."

---

*Working in pastry has been a means for Andrea to support her true passion—art, and she finds time in between her pastry-chef demands to work on it. Her current area of focus is sewing, and she is making miniature trousseaus (small doll-like outfits) using creative materials. She has also worked with other media, including oil painting and sculpture. Her art is displayed in museums throughout the country. "It's so much about who I am. It's just very challenging to me, and it's just very satisfying."

Job Challenges
"I'm used to working in a place where people are trained and everything is taken very seriously." When Andrea's work environment lacks professionalism, it frustrates her. • It can be stressful dealing with management.

Steps to Current Job
- The Art Institute of Chicago, Bachelor of Arts in Painting and Textile Design.
- Construction Laborer for two years.
- Decided to learn a trade that would support her art. Attended The Cooking and Hospitality Institute of Chicago Pastry School for one year.
- Has worked in pastry for the past 13 years in restaurants and bakeries.

Advice
Andrea does not believe that it is necessary to go to the most exclusive or expensive pastry school to study, and she says, "Certainly work in a restaurant first before you go to school for it." As far as where to work, it really depends on your temperament. Andrea works for a small bakery, which she finds less stressful than working in a restaurant. Her main focus at the bakery is production. As a pastry chef for a restaurant, "Your focus is the plate... and having it complement the meal." She describes working in a restaurant as fast-paced and exciting, but also emotional and stressful. She also says that the size of the place where you work determines what your job entails. Andrea participates more in production than if she were at a larger facility.

"I would just really try something... give it a few years. If you are interested in it, see if it's something you can work with. Don't just give up because you don't like your job at one place or because you have a bad boss."

Helpful Personality Traits
Driven, possess a good food palate, intense, enjoy physical work, workaholic mentality, and good hand-to-eye coordination.

Hobbies & Interests
Sewing, road trips, and dinners with friends.

Angela M. Brown

Opera Singer

{ *"Nothing is beneath you, sing, sing, sing!"* }

Opera singer Angela Brown is tickled to see her name on the SOLD OUT sign for AIDA in front of the Metropolitan Opera.   **Courtesy of JEJ Artists.**

Job Description

As an opera singer, Angela sings a story. Everything in an opera is set to music, and all of the words are sung. She performs as a principal artist in operas and as a guest performer at different venues around the world.

A Day on the Job

Starts with physical exercise to warm up her body and to get in touch with her core singing muscles. • Exercises her voice by vocalizing and working with a vocal coach in preparation for her upcoming events. • Mentally studies her music. • Communicates with her agent to determine when and where her next

performance will occur, travel arrangements, and payment for performances.
• Sometimes conducts master classes for opera students, usually in the towns
where she is performing.

Job Likes
Angela likes the travel involved with her job. Her job takes her all over the world,
from Venice, Italy, to small towns in America. • "I love to dig into a character"
when singing in an opera. Finding the "back story" is fun.

Job Challenges
Travel can also be a negative aspect to Angela's job. It is hard to establish and
keep relationships going when you are gone a lot. • The life of an opera singer is
expensive. The costumes, competition fees, and travel all add up.

Steps to Current Job
- Indiana Vocational Technical School—Worked as a hospital dietary aide for
  one year and a secretary for two years while attending school.
- Oakwood College in Huntsville, Alabama, Bachelor of Arts in Music.
  Started the Positive Images singing group.
- Indiana University in Bloomington—graduate work in classics while work-
  ing as vocal coach for the IU Soul Review.
- Started touring with Dean Charles Webb of Indiana University School of
  Music.
- Began entering competitions, which helped support her financially and
  brought her notoriety. Among her accomplishments are winner of the
  Metropolitan Opera National Council Auditions and shared first prize at
  the Altamura/Enrico Caruso International Voice Competition in Gibraltar.
- Opera Singer—sings at venues worldwide, including the Metropolitan
  Opera; Indianapolis Opera; San Antonio Symphony; Teatro La Fenice in
  Venice, Italy; The Kennedy Center; and Opera Company of Philadelphia.
  CDs recorded include opera arias, art songs, African-American spirituals,
  and selections from *Porgy and Bess*.

Advice
Besides having the talent, a good teacher is a necessity. Your teacher should have
opera knowledge and experience and be current in today's teaching practices. She
also says that you must "sing all the time," because you've got to "oil the
machine." Sing anywhere, anytime someone asks you; "Nothing is beneath you,
sing, sing, sing!" As far as educating yourself, there are many, many schools where
you can study opera. She suggests attending one of the top opera schools in the
country, along the lines of Julliard; Indiana University; University of Kentucky;
Curtis Institute and Academy of Vocal Arts, both of which are in Philadelphia;
or the Manhattan School of Music.

Angela says young women should focus on the goal. She doesn't understand why young people get caught up in sex, drinking, and drugs when all that does is complicate things and takes you further away from where you want to be. "Keep your eyes on your goal," and stay grounded.

Helpful Personality Traits

Confident, assertive, hard worker, possess integrity, flexible and kind—"It costs nothing to be kind."

Hobbies & Interests

Makeup artistry, reading, sewing, crafts, and interior decorating.

READ IT ALL!

You have the luxury of exploring without boundaries. So, don't limit yourself to reading just those profiles that catch your eye. We purposely organized these jobs by first name rather than by career. Learning about the many different sides of each job will help you formulate your own career and desired lifestyle. Take, for example, Wanda Revis, the community college nursing instructor (see page 230). Maybe nursing is not for you, but the lifestyle of an instructor might be.

You can learn from each Firestarter whether her job interests you or not. If something does "spark" your interest, why not search the Internet for more information about that job? It's amazing what you can find. A site that we found enormously useful is the Occupational Outlook Handbook on the U.S. Department of Labor's Web site, www.bls.gov/oco. Once you have an overview of a particular job, you'll feel more comfortable taking some of the next steps for exploring careers:

- Someone in your school's career center or your guidance counselor can direct you to helpful resources.
- Talk with your parents and their friends. Chances are they'll know someone in the field that interests you and how to get in touch with him or her and learn more.
- A career assessment test can help identify your interests and strengths and can guide you in a direction of possible career choices. You can find these at your school's career center, libraries, on the Internet, and in bookstores.

continued

continued

- Libraries and librarians are wonderful resources. Check out books about the careers that interest you, or ask a librarian how best to research a company where you think you'd like to work.
- Contact your local community college to see whether it has a career center that you can visit.
- Volunteer in the field(s) that interest you. This is one of the best ways to find out what a job is really like. Make a phone call or send an e-mail to someone in your field of interest and ask whether you can help them out after school or during breaks.
- Interview someone in your field of interest. Call or e-mail him or her to set up an informational interview.
- Learn from the Firestarters in this book. These are real women who were once just where you are.

Angela Carr

Massage Therapist

{ *"This is a great job if you want to work with famous people, or if you want to work on a cruise ship or go to Aspen and work in a resort."* }

Job Description
Angela helps people relax and relieves muscular tension through touch and by strategically manipulating their muscles.

A Day on the Job
Returns phone calls and sets up appointments. • Purchases supplies, such as lotion, linens, and water for clients. • Does laundry. Many massage therapists use a laundry service for massage-table linens and towels, but Angela says, "It costs a lot to send them out." • Cleans massage room between appointments. "If I need to vacuum or dust, I might do something like that." • Does all accounting/banking necessary for her business. • Sends out marketing newsletter to potential and

existing clients. • Interacts with clients prior to massage to determine what areas of the body need more attention. • Typically performs three to four one-hour massages each day. Angela says that four is the maximum that she is willing to do because she does deep-tissue massage, which is physically demanding.

Job Likes
"I have a lot of freedom, and I like that, but my job is only flexible because I work for myself. If you work in a day spa or a chiropractor's office, you have a boss… you wouldn't be as flexible. And, I don't have employees… so I feel pretty free. I can come and go pretty easily." • "I don't have to work a lot, and I still make a decent amount of money. It's almost like a part-time job." • "I like the people [clients]. I'm just so appreciative that they're there, so I just love them." • "People really enjoy massage, so it's rewarding."

Job Challenges
Because Angela works for herself, "There are no benefits. I don't have a 401K [retirement fund] that is matched by an employer." Insurance is also a big expense. • "If I'm not working, I'm not making money." • "I wish that I worked with more co-workers."

Steps to Current Job
- Georgia State University in Atlanta, Bachelor of Science in Psychology.
- Atlanta School of Massage, Certified Massage Therapist.
- Licensed nationally and in North Carolina.
- Massage Therapist.

Advice
Angela says, "Go to a reputable massage school." She also says to use the career as a way to travel. "This is a great job if you want to work with famous people, or if you want to work on a cruise ship or go to Aspen and work in a resort." When you want to settle down, work for someone else first, like a chiropractor, day spa, or gym; then you can build your own clientele and work for yourself.

"You've gotta pick something you love because it shines through—your enthusiasm and your passion—and people can tell if you love your job or if you hate your job. You just go so much further when you enjoy what you're doing."

Helpful Personality Traits
Business minded, nurturing, accepting of people, physically fit, desire to help people, and likeable.

Hobbies & Interests
Playing guitar, singing, snow skiing, and going to the beach.

Angela Kilpatrick

Commercial Airline Pilot

> *"It is unique, and it does make you feel good when you go to work and people say 'Oh there's a lady pilot.'"*

Job Description
Angela is a pilot for a commercial airline. She is a first officer pilot, second in command to the captain.

A Day on the Job
The day before her scheduled flights, Angela flies from her home in North Carolina to Chicago, where she is based. "You can't call in and say, 'It snowed three feet at my house or my flight is canceled.' They don't accept that. You can live where you want to, but there is no excuse for not getting to work." • The morning of her flight, Angela gets to the airport an hour and a half before the departure time, usually around 4 a.m. She is required to sign in at least an hour before departure, and "We go through security just like everybody else." • Performs preflight checks, along with the maintenance crew, both inside the cockpit and outside the airplane. • Puts the flight plan into the computer while the passengers are loading. • Flies three to five 90-minute "legs," also known as flights, per day. • Spends the night in a hotel. She is usually gone three days per week or 10 to 15 days per month. • Catches a flight home after three days of flying. • Attends training programs to keep her skills up-to-date.

Job Likes
"It is unique, and it does make you feel good when you go to work and people say 'Oh there's a lady pilot.'" • Angela has a lot of flexibility with her schedule. She is able to decide when and where she flies. The more seniority pilots have, the more say they have with their schedules. • "It's fun."

Job Challenges
"Being away from home." • Because the airline industry is in turmoil, Angela finds the job security and pay level "just not what it used to be."

Steps to Current Job
- Started flying lessons in high school.
- University of South Carolina, in Columbia, Bachelor of Science in Business Administration. Attended flight school during college.
- Commuter airline pilot for one and a half years.
- Air-traffic controller for five years.
- Commuter airline pilot for one and a half years.
- Commercial airline pilot for 15 years; currently taking a leave of absence while raising her young child.

Advice
Most airlines require you to have a bachelor's degree to be a pilot. Your bachelor's degree does not have to be in aviation, but there are some colleges that offer aviation programs. Learning to fly is expensive. If you can't afford to pay for lessons, an alternative way to learn is to join the military. Although Angela did not take the military route, she acknowledges that most of her colleagues did. "It's hard getting there. It took a long time to get to the major airline." Angela doesn't want to discourage young women, but she does think that it's important to know there are many requirements that must be fulfilled before becoming a commercial airline pilot, such as completing many hours of flying and passing physical and written examinations. (See the U.S. Department of Labor's Bureau of Labor Statistics Web site for more information on job requirements: http://stats.bls.gov/oco/ocos107.htm.)

"I think you have to realize, that because you are a female... you are a lot of times held to a higher standard, not given the benefit of the doubt. But as long as you do your job and do it well, it's a great career." According to the organization Women in Aviation International (www.wai.org/resources/facts.cfm), women represent only six percent of the total pilot population.

Helpful Personality Traits
Assertive, confident, decisive, and able to work well with others.

Hobbies & Interests
Running and exercise.

Ann Person

Chief Operating Officer (COO)

{ *"I love everything about my job."* }

Job Description
Ann's job is to oversee all of the functions and employees of the insurance company where she works, making sure that everything is running efficiently and effectively.

A Day on the Job
Writes business plans to set up operations (accounting, human resources, information technology, and so on) in the company. • Approves final vendor selections for all business equipment and software (for example, computers, telephones, faxes, and copy machines) necessary for efficient office operations and policy and *claim* management. • Evaluates and analyzes data (such as *premiums*, losses, and claims against policies) to help determine whether changes are needed within the company. • Analyzes trends within the industry to determine where to concentrate marketing efforts. • Comes up with and participates in team-building tasks for employees and says, "I talk to employees daily to build camaraderie in the company." • Handles any personnel issues, such as hiring, firing, and disciplinary action.

Job Likes
"I love everything about my job—no one thing. I like all the different aspects; probably, I guess, the variety. It's always new things, different things. It's always changing."

Job Challenges
Even when pressed, Ann couldn't think of anything that she dislikes about her job. She attributes that to the team of people working with her. "If we get anybody who comes in with an attitude, wanting to sour our apples, we're going to send them out the door."

Steps to Current Job
- North Carolina State University in Raleigh, Bachelor of Science in Chemical Engineering.
- Chemical Engineer for three years.
- Assistant Administrator for 10 years.
- Vice President, COO for insurance company.

Advice
"Get the best education you can." Ann says that your degree doesn't necessarily have to be in the field where you ultimately hope to work. "It helped me obviously, being a chemical engineer, that people perceive you as smart." Ultimately, a degree that is structured but covers a breadth of topics, such as an MBA or an engineering degree, will help you be a good COO. Ann also thinks that you should think about entering an industry that has staying power, such as insurance or health care. "People are always going to need insurance, and people are always going to be sick."

"Be confident in yourself, and be your own person and not let peer pressure bother you. Set the standard. Don't follow it."

Helpful Personality Traits
Detail oriented, organized, and likes to build things.

Hobbies & Interests
Playing the piano, cross-stitching, needlepoint, crocheting, and her dogs.

Premiums are the fees that people pay each month to their insurance company to ensure coverage.

A *claim* is a form that an insured person submits to his or her insurance company when he or she has had something lost, stolen, or damaged, requesting funds in accordance with his or her insurance policy.

Ann B. Ross

Writer

{ *"I like the idea of writing because it's a world that I can escape into."* }

Job Description

Ann is a writer of fiction. Her most recent novels are the *Miss Julia* series, of which the first in the series was **Miss Julia Speaks Her Mind.** At press time, she had written six books in the series and was contracted with her publisher to complete one book each year.

A Day on the Job

Writes approximately three to four hours a day—"I have some coffee... and then I go right to the computer." • Communicates with her agent about the business end of selling her books. • Returns e-mails from her Web site, www.missjulia.com. • Sends newsletters to those on her *Miss Julia* mailing list. • Promotes her book approximately two months out of the year. "My publisher sets up a tour each year, right at the time that a new book comes out." The tour entails traveling to bookstores for book signings, speaking about her book, reading excerpts from it, and signing autographs. She also makes radio and television appearances.

Job Likes

"I like the idea of writing because it's a world that I can escape into. It's a world that I build, and I can put whatever people I want in it and have whatever happen that I want, although a lot of times they [the characters] surprise me!" • "I like to work alone. I do like the quiet, the silence, just the peace of being here and working by myself." Although the writing routine is introverted, the promotion of her book provides her with a more extroverted outlet, giving her a nice balance between the two. • "It's been amazing to me that these books have been so effective for so many people." Ann remembers a story of a fan who told her that her sister had read these books during chemotherapy, and it was the first time her sister had laughed out loud in over a year. • "It's a real thrill to walk into a bookstore and see a line out on the sidewalk." Ann finds promoting the book exciting and fun, but the schedule can also be tiring.

Job Challenges

"The business end, and that's why I am so thankful to have a good agent." Ann feels fortunate to have an agent who looks out for her best interests and takes care of negotiations with her publisher.

Steps to Current Job

- South Carolina Baptist Hospital in Columbia, nursing program.
- Operating room registered nurse for five years.
- Armstrong College in Savannah, Georgia, general college courses.
- Blue Ridge Technical College in Hendersonville, North Carolina; took a writing class while raising her family.
- University of North Carolina at Asheville, Bachelor of Arts in Literature.
- Wrote two murder mysteries, *The Murder Cure* and *The Murder Stroke*.
- University of North Carolina at Chapel Hill, Master of Arts in English; wrote *The Pilgrimage*.
- University of North Carolina at Chapel Hill, Ph.D. in English; field of study was Medieval English Literature and Language.
- Professor at University of North Carolina at Asheville in Literature and Humanities.
- Writer of the *Miss Julia* novels.

Advice

A liberal arts degree is a great background for a writer. Study what interests you. The more experience and knowledge you acquire, the more you have to draw upon for your writing. She feels that "If you really want to write, you maybe don't need any formal classes in writing. You can learn the skills, but not the talent, of writing from the public library. I really think the books I read from there were more help than any writing class I had."

Ann suggests that if you don't know what you want to study in college, you should get a liberal arts degree. "With a good, rounded humanities or liberal arts degree, you can do most anything you want to." When she was a young woman, the two main career paths she felt were acceptable for a woman were nursing and teaching. "There are so many opportunities now that I did not feel were open to me." Ann adds, "Don't get married young." She explains that it is more difficult to follow your dreams when you are married and have a family at a young age.

Helpful Personality Traits

Disciplined, self-starter, good observer of others, good ear for speech patterns, introspective of self and others, and enjoy telling a story.

Hobbies & Interests

Reading, needlepoint, horseback riding, and spending time with family.

Anna Barbrey Joiner

Performing Violist and Professor of Music

{ *"Musical training and years of undergraduate and graduate school approach the same intensity and commitment of those entering the legal or medical professions."* }

Job Description

Anna performs regularly as a violist, as a soloist, a chamber player, and a member of various orchestras. She is a Professor of Viola and Music Education at Furman University in Greenville, South Carolina. In addition to teaching privately in her home, Anna is the Director of the Instrumental Program at a private middle school. Each summer she is a performing artist and member of the faculty for a major music festival. "It takes a lot of coordination of schedules to balance several jobs, performing, and a family."

A Day on the Job

Starts her day teaching a music-education class at the university. • Teaches two or three private viola lessons to college students. • Travels to the middle school and teaches several classes of strings and coordinates instrumental activities with other music and arts teachers. • Teaches private lessons at home after picking up her daughter from high school. • Performs in public concerts at the university, at the middle school, or with a professional musical group three to four times each month. "The fall and winter, especially December, are extremely busy for musicians." • Teaches and performs at a major music festival each summer for seven weeks.

Job Likes

"Music takes me to so many different places and provides the opportunity to meet a variety of people. Music has opened so many doors to a richer life." • "I enjoy every aspect of the variety of musical activities required in my work."

Job Challenges

"It takes a tremendous amount of mental and emotional focus and concentration. You must have good organizational and planning skills, always be prepared, and be calm under pressure."

Steps to Current Job

- Furman University in Greenville, South Carolina, Bachelor of Music in Violin Performance.
- The Florida State University in Tallahassee, Master of Music degree in Violin Performance.
- The Florida State University, Master of Music degree in Music Education.
- The Florida State University, Doctor of Music in Viola Performance.
- University of Georgia in Athens, Associate Professor of Music and Director of the UGA Talent Education Center (pre-college Suzuki string program). Taught at UGA for 10 years.
- Furman University, Greenville, South Carolina, Professor of Viola and Music Education for 11 years; Director of Instrumental Music at Christ Church Episcopal School in Greenville, South Carolina; and summers on the Artist-Faculty of the Brevard Music Center in Brevard, North Carolina.

Advice

"Young music students must spend the time necessary to develop their skills and technique. Believe it or not, when you get older and have a family and have a job, there is often very little time to practice. You have to rely a lot of times on those early years of solid technical training." Speaking from experience, Anna suggests "In music, there are many avenues and career paths. Often a young person has to just keep working and experimenting until you find what fits." Anna began her studies as a violinist. After a summer of experimenting with the viola, she discovered that the viola suited her better. "I love the lower, richer sound of the instrument." She also points out that "A person who aspires to teach music at the university level usually needs a doctorate in order to successfully move through the ranks of promotion and tenure. Musical training and years of undergraduate and graduate school approach the same intensity and commitment of those entering the legal or medical professions."

A verse in the Bible, Romans 12:1 and 2, touches Anna. "This verse stuck with me a long time ago. I think young women, and women in general, feel like we have to do what society tells us to do. This Bible passage is appropriate for young women embarking on their life journey because it instructs the reader to 'not conform yourselves to the standards of this world.'"

Helpful Personality Traits

Natural curiosity about all kinds of music, enjoy people, patience, tolerance, and a love of music.

Hobbies & Interests

Relaxing with reading, looking through catalogs, and watching movies as an escape.

"Be who you are and say what you feel, because those who mind don't matter, and those who matter, don't mind."

—Dr. Seuss

Annette Simon

Advertising Creative Director/Art Director

{ *"It's fun. Honestly, we get to play."* }

Job Description

Annette works for an advertising agency coming up with concepts to convey ideas about a product through different advertising media—TV, radio, magazine, newspaper, and so on. Once the concept is determined, Annette is responsible for figuring out the visual look of the advertising. As a Creative Director, Annette also mentors and oversees the work of creative teams that work for her.

A Day on the Job

Receives a *job brief* and researches product(s) on which she and her partner (writer) will be working. "We're given an assignment, say, to sell a particular kind of car. So, we find out who are the people buying the car and what they like and what we can honestly say about the car." • Concepts/brainstorms ideas with partner and makes sure that the ideas are solid and can work for a *campaign*. "We have fun. We sit together and think of ideas." • Oversees and mentors other teams of writers and art directors. "Creative Directors get to say, 'This is a great idea. Let's keep pushing this,' or 'maybe we're not quite there yet. Let's see if there's something we haven't tried or thought of.'" • Works on a computer designing the look and feel of print layouts or television commercials. • Gets input from clients regarding campaign ideas.

Job Likes

"It's fun. Honestly, we get to play." • "We learn new stuff every day." Annette worked with a national chain of Italian restaurants and says, "I knew nothing about Italian food or restaurants or how restaurants work; and now we get to see it all the way through from why they would hire somebody to why they pick this particular plate of ravioli."

Job Challenges

"Most creative people have sensitive egos because of what we're producing… you can't help that it's an expression of your talent. A lot of times it is a competition. If your idea doesn't sell this time, it's not a bad thing. Keep going. The best creative directors are open to suggestions, ideas, and criticisms from others."

Steps to Current Job

- University of Cincinnati, Ohio, Bachelor of Science in Design; Annette's program was set up so that she could go to school a quarter and then work a quarter. This co-op program allowed her to build up her resume. During this time, she worked as a Graphic Designer for different companies.
- Advertising Art Director for 13 years.
- Advertising Senior Art Director for one year.
- Advertising Associate Creative Director for two years.
- Creative Director for five years. Annette recently decided to stop working for a while to be at home with her sons and says, "At 15 and 11, they seem to need me now more than they did when they were little."

Advice

Annette says that there are "ad schools" today where advertising agencies look for their future art directors and copywriters. Once you enter the field, "Don't be afraid of working long hours… it doesn't mean that every moment of your life is going to be filled with work, but you are going to have to work some weekends, especially in the beginning."

Helpful Personality Traits

Always doodling, looks at things differently, and observant.

Hobbies & Interests

Children's books (Annette is a published author/illustrator).

A *campaign* is a central idea that can be used for any number of media.

A *job brief* is a report from account services given to the creative team that gives them the details necessary to come up with ideas. It may include, among other things, product details, client mandates, and deadlines.

Anne Valentine

Landscape Architect

> *"Because what we do has to do with change, it's all disturbance in some way. But we look at it always from the standpoint of what do we do to protect the land?"*

Job Description

Anne designs outdoor spaces and neighborhoods, making them functional and attractive. "We help people shape the land for different uses." Her job includes analyzing the land for its environment and potential; grading design, which includes erosion control; site design; and finally, designing the look of the final space—"the stuff that people think of as landscape architecture, which is planting, doing gardens, doing the landscaping." She works mostly designing planned communities, but landscape architects also design for private homes, parks (including theme parks and national parks), malls, office buildings, golf courses, and so on.

A Day on the Job

Works on different projects in various stages of progress. Working part-time while raising her small children, Anne is able to work on approximately six projects at a time. • Meets with clients. "A lot of the jobs we work on are large pieces of property. We'll go out with a client when there's nothing there but woods and walk around and figure out how they can use the property." • Draws designs by hand and on the computer. "Part of the reason I got into it was liking to draw and design." • Consults with other landscape architects in her office and many other consultants, such as civil engineers, ecologists, architects, and contractors.

Job Likes

Anne likes that her work combines her love for art and the outdoors. Living in the mountains of western North Carolina, hiking various properties is a big part of her job. She also enjoys the artistry involved with landscape design, especially drawing her initial design ideas by hand. • "It's a neat field because the other people who do it are so interesting." • "Every project is always different—different size, different scope, different things that you are trying to achieve—and that makes it fun because you don't get bored."

Job Challenges

"Each project and client are unique and that's hard because you are never doing the same thing twice. There can be a lot of time pressure to it because you are always meeting somebody else's deadlines."

Steps to Current Job

- Wellesley College in Boston, Massachusetts, Bachelor of Arts with a double major in English and Art History.
- Graphic Designer for five years.
- North Carolina State University in Raleigh, Master of Landscape Architecture (MLA).
- Landscape Architect. Anne points out that in her state of North Carolina, an internship period and passing a three-day exam are required to be a licensed landscape architect.

Advice

Anne suggests looking at the many components of landscape architecture and exploring your interests by working in that area. During summer breaks, find a job in forestry, construction, nurseries, or landscaping. Go and learn about the aspects that interest you. For example, "If the forestry part of it, the plants or the trees interest you, then go and learn about that." She also suggests visiting people working in landscape architecture and talking to them about their jobs.

"I was so good about doing what my teachers wanted me to do and doing what my parents wanted me to do, that I think it took me a long time to figure out what I wanted to do." You really need to take yourself seriously and determine what exactly it is that makes you happy, not just follow the comfortable route. Working as a Graphic Designer, Anne says, "I got really tired of sitting inside in front of a computer." She decided that landscape architecture fit her personality better and went back to school.

Helpful Personality Traits

Enjoys the outdoors, artistic, curious, environmentally conscious, a people person and interested in how things interrelate.

Hobbies & Interests

Art, hiking, sailing, and travel (also beneficial for her job because you learn by observation).

NETWORKING

Firestarters is an excellent example of networking. We asked family, friends, colleagues, and friends of friends to help us with this book. Yes, these women had busy schedules, yet they made time to talk with us.

Ask your parents, teachers, and other adults in fields that interest you if you can volunteer, spend a day on the job, or just talk with them. We think that you'll find a warm reception like we did. You'll make valuable contacts, gain experience, and maybe even find a mentor. Speaking to the right person can open doors that were closed to you before.

Annie Harvey

Correctional Warden of the North Carolina Correctional Institution for Women

"Success to me is living each day better than you lived yesterday, and when you have a 17-year-old who has been sentenced to life without parole, just assisting her to live within the confines of this prison, I think that's a success."

Warden Annie Harvey checks her e-mail before heading into one of her numerous meetings.

Job Description

Annie says, "My responsibility is to provide hope to the hopeless." She works for a prison "that houses female offenders who have sentences anywhere from a death sentence to misdemeanor charges, and some who have not been sentenced yet." Annie goes on to explain that this institution is her state's "major facility for the female offender." They have a 24-hour infirmary and 24-hour mental facility "that houses chronic and acute inmates," and her prison also processes all female felons before they are placed in other prisons. She oversees all of this as well as all other operations of the prison (personnel, maintenance, and any inmate issues).

A Day on the Job

Attends lots of meetings. "I meet all the time. In the course of the day, I may talk with my Medical Director, nurses, psychologists, psychiatrists." • Plans programs with program staff. "To give you an example, today at 6 o'clock, we have a gospel group that's coming." Annie tells how her staff had to change the location of a performance due to excessive heat and lack of air conditioning. • Handles all personnel issues—pay, performance, complaints, hiring, and so on. • Deals with any inmates' concerns or disciplinary issues. "Inmates write me all the time—complaints, concerns, so I may talk to staff to find out if their complaints are valid and if so what we need to do to take corrective action." • Talks with the state's Attorney General's office when suits are filed against the prison by inmates. • Sets the budget and ensures that the prison has the equipment and resources to run efficiently. • Walks the prison grounds. "The inmates are not afraid to come up and say, 'Hey Miss Harvey. Let me tell you this. Let me tell you that.' It takes me a long time to get from point A to point B."

Job Likes

"I like the fact that I have an opportunity to provide hope to people who are generally considered hopeless and to assist them in changing their lives. Female population [inmates], they're willing to change, and that's what I like about it." • Annie says that she doesn't follow inmates' stories once they leave, but she enjoys helping them achieve a certain amount of success while at her prison. "Success to me is living each day better than you lived yesterday, and when you have a 17-year-old who has been sentenced to life without parole, just assisting her to live within the confines of this prison, I think that's a success."

Job Challenges

"I do not like the pay. I think that correctional employees are underpaid. It takes a very unique person to work with a group of people who everybody else says they can't manage. We have over 1,000 [people] who are not law-abiding. I do not like the fact that we manage people who the FBI [Federal Bureau of

Investigation] and the SBI [State Bureau of Investigation] say are dangerous…
but when they [the inmates] get here, nobody thinks they're dangerous anymore.
Our staff does not receive the credit or respect for the complexity of their jobs.
I don't like that."

Steps to Current Job
- Held positions of Sergeant and Officer at the North Carolina Correctional Institution for Women for a total of six years.
- Shaw University, Raleigh, North Carolina, Bachelor of Science in Public Administration.
- Captain (in charge of training and transportation) at the North Carolina Correctional Institution for Women for three years.
- Superintendent of a correctional facility for one year—Annie was sent to get this facility up and running.
- Deputy Warden at the North Carolina Correctional Institution for Women for two years and was promoted to her current position of Warden.

Advice
Annie thinks that any job experiences that you've previously held can help you if you want to pursue a career in corrections. She says, "No matter what you do, do your best, even if you are working at a fast-food restaurant. Do your best because you are gaining skills. You learn how to interact with people. You learn how to count money. Anything that you learn in any other area can be utilized in corrections."

When it comes to getting through day-to-day of life, Annie says, "Junior high and high school, they're very trying times, and I think that's a time to begin to learn who you are… to find value in who you are and what makes you different from other people." Don't follow the crowd—do what you really want to do. "Don't go to the park, when you really want to go to the movies. It's those small choices that you learn as you develop that will assist you in making better choices later, and it is better to make mistakes on small choices than to make them on big choices."

Helpful Personality Traits
Annie says that just about every personality type is needed in corrections, but the ability to be fair, consistent, and firm is very important.

Hobbies & Interests
"I like *Lifetime*" [Television Network], gardening, inspirational books and music, painting, and stained glass.

Annie Meadows

Sales Consultant for a Hair Products Distributor

{ *"Anything a salon needs, I sell."* }

Annie Meadows, a sales consultant for a hair-products distributor, checks to make sure her client is well stocked.

Job Description
Annie helps hair salons grow their businesses by determining which products fit their needs and the needs of their clients.

A Day on the Job
Visits salons to find out what products they need as well as any problems or concerns they have. "For some it's education, some it's sales, some it's staffing. I try and find out what their concerns are and problem-solve." • Promotes products through demonstrations and samples. • Encourages education. Hairdressers in the state where Annie works have to have eight hours of credit in continuing education, and her company sponsors classes. "I answer questions if I can, but I also try and get them to go to classes." • Fields phone calls from clients. • Orders products for clients. "Anything a salon needs, I sell."

Job Likes
"I like working with the people—the hairdressers." • "I like the flexibility of my schedule... the direction that we try and steer their business is at my own discretion."

Job Challenges
"Our sales meetings are brutal. We have sales meetings once a month and they're just... boring." The company where Annie works has been bought out several times, and she feels, "There's no real direction in our company anymore. It's kind of up to us to figure it out."

Steps to Current Job
- Appalachian State University, Boone, North Carolina, Bachelor of Science in Psychology.
- Human Resource Benefits Coordinator for a hospital for five years.
- Recruiter for a recruiting firm for 10 years.
- Manager for a recruiting Web site for three months.
- Sales Consultant.

Advice
Positions are limited in the sales field where Annie works. She suggests, "Network... it's not a job that you're going to find in the newspaper. You need to really talk to your salon owner to see who they use, who they like. In my experience, most of the better jobs you find by networking and not through the newspaper."

No matter what career you choose, Annie says simple work-ethic rules are worth remembering. "Always show up 10 minutes early for work... you can be the slowest person to pick up on new things, but if you're there 10 minutes early every day, your boss is going to like you."

Helpful Personality Traits
Outgoing, good listener, self starter, and diligent.

Hobbies & Interests
Walking her dogs, reading fiction, working out, gardening, house projects, and entertaining.

Barbara Whitecross

Certified Wedding Consultant

{ *"The wedding consultant is the liaison between the bride and all of the vendors, sometimes the bride and her mother, sometimes the bride and the fiancé."* }

Job Description

Barbara helps brides plan their weddings. She says, "The wedding consultant is the liaison between the bride and all of the vendors (hotel, caterer, florist, bridal salon, etc.), sometimes the bride and her mother, sometimes the bride and the fiancé. She works for the bride to make sure that everything happens the way the bride wants it." Barbara started her business in Bermuda, and the majority of the weddings she helps plan take place there. Because most of the couples she helps are from out of town, she describes these types of weddings as "destination weddings." Barbara employs a team of people that help her coordinate all of the wedding-day details because she does not live in Bermuda anymore. "They are the ones who are actually holding the bride's hand throughout the process."

A Day on the Job

"Meets" with bride over the phone to find out what type of wedding she wants. • Starts working on tracking down a location for the wedding and prices for all of the wedding details (flowers, cake, caterer, location, music, and so on). "We find out what it is that she wants, and is it going to be feasible. If she wants a wedding at the beach, maybe not everything that's available at her hometown is going to be available at the beach." • Makes sure someone on her team visits the church or the location of the wedding. • Talks with the minister or officiant to determine whether there are any special requirements. • Secures the marriage certificate if necessary. • Attends the wedding-gown fitting with the bride if she lives in the same area as Barbara. "Some of the brides don't have their mothers here… so, they ask us to go along and give an honest, objective opinion."

Job Likes

"I like the flexibility." • "I like that I'm never doing the same thing two days in a row. I get to talk to people from all over the world, and I'm learning about the cultures, different religions… so we've done a lot of weddings where I've had no idea what was involved—Indian weddings, Jewish weddings."

Job Challenges

"I don't get to meet my brides from the destination weddings. Sometimes I'll go through a year and a half dealing with them on the phone twice a week, and I'll never have met them." Prices seem to have skyrocketed in the 21 years that Barbara has been doing this, and she says, "The average budget cannot accommodate what the bride wants or what her sister or friends had; so 'running away to be married' is becoming very popular."

Steps to Current Job

- Three years of study between Boston University and Suffolk University, both in Boston, Massachusetts.
- Secretary in Bermuda for four years—"I got an offer I couldn't refuse... I wanted a change... I was 22."
- Completed correspondence course through the National Association of Certified Wedding Consultants (now defunct, but absorbed by the Association of Bridal Consultants) to become a certified wedding planner.
- Owner/Operator of a wedding boutique for eight years and wedding consultant for 21 years.
- Sold the boutique but continued to be a wedding consultant.
- Meredith College in Raleigh, North Carolina; Bachelor of Science in Interior Design. While working on her degree, Barbara has worked full-time as a wedding planner, and plans to continue the business now that she's graduated.

Advice

Barbara says to get an internship with a wedding consultant, but be prepared to do more listening than active work. "I've had a couple of people work with me in the office, but it's very hard to send someone to do something because the people want to deal with me. They know me." She recommends that you go to the Association of Bridal Consultants (ABC) Web site. "They have a very cohesive Web site. They have all of the information about taking the [certification] course," and Barbara thinks that it's very important to get the certification and to join the ABC. "It definitely makes you more credible. It also gives you a whole organization behind you."

When speaking of her teenage, early-college years, Barbara says, "That was a terrible time in my life because I could not figure out what I wanted to do, and I couldn't understand how all of my friends knew what they wanted to be. I thought there was something wrong with me." She thinks that you should try and get your general college courses out of the way—courses you would have to have regardless of what career you choose. This will give you time to decide what you really want. Barbara explains, "Figure out what it is you want to do, if you can, and just go for it. Don't let anybody tell you that you can't do it. Everything's open to us."

Helpful Personality Traits

Outgoing, sure of yourself, able to talk with strangers, and assertive.

Hobbies & Interests

Sewing, needlepoint, helping friends decorate, and spending time with family.

Learn more about Barbara's business at www.bermudaweddingsalon.com.

Beth Hockman

Organic Blueberry Farmer and Future Importer/Exporter of African Arts and Crafts*

{ *"I tell you what, the monkeys are pesty little things, and if the entire orchard was not encased in netting they would engorge themselves."* }

Beth Hockman serves up dessert at a staff party celebrating the end of blueberry-picking season.

Job Description

Beth and her husband manage an organic blueberry farm in South Africa.

A Day on the Job

Picking Season (December—February)

Twelve-hour days overseeing the picking, sorting, weighing, and packaging of blueberries. "All of the workers are Sotho. We are in their tribal land. During picking season we will have close to 60 women working for us." • Office work—including tracking the workers' hours and the amount of blueberries each employee picked, payroll and passing out wages to employees, and invoicing the buyer. • Delivers the blueberries to exporters. • Consults with an agent to ensure that they get the best market price.

Non-Picking Months and Year-Round

Cares for berries through pruning, weeding, irrigation, covering them for protection from hail and monkeys, and applying various organic farming treatments, including *biodynamic farming* methods. • Manages customer accounts. • Budgets for the next year. • Finds new markets for the blueberries. • Prepares for the European organic audit to qualify for European organic certification. "They certify us before every picking season, making sure the organic standards are met each year."

Job Likes

Beth likes being outdoors. When she worked in public education, she found, "After having nature as your classroom, four walls [were] stifling." • "It is amazing to do work that aids in poverty alleviation in a developing country. Many of the women who work for us during the three months of picking support their families for the entire year on the money earned." • "Learning about organic farming and blueberries." • Beth enjoys working with people from the Sotho tribe. "I like working beside them because they are happy, colorful, vibrant people. They have a respect for life that supersedes any materialism of America."

Job Challenges

"The isolation! A farm in Africa is extremely isolated." She misses things that we take for granted, such as movie theatres, bookstores, family, "driving on the right side of the road, and yummy chocolate-chip cookies." • "I also struggle at times with the sexism of both the white and black South African cultures." Beth finds both cultures to be very patriarchal. • Her work environment differs from one in America. "I miss having a work environment with a strong female support system and network. I miss working in a place where I understand the language being spoken and I miss lunch with lots of co-workers."

Steps to Current Job

- Michigan State University in East Lansing, Bachelor of Science in Psychology with a minor in Parks and Recreation.
- Minnesota State University in Mankato, Master of Science in Experiential Education with additional coursework in women's studies.
- Outdoor Educator with numerous outdoor schools, such as Outward Bound, for 10 years.
- High school government, Spanish, and health teacher for one year.
- Substitute teacher for one year.
- Blueberry farm manager.

Advice

"Pick a job you love, and you will never work a day in your life. Try all sorts of things and try them when you're young. There will be plenty of time for the house, car, 2.5 kids. Live big, bold, yet humbly. Care for others, and find mission in your work."

Helpful Personality Traits

Love of the outdoors, like physical work, disciplined, adventurous, willing to live within another culture, confident and a sense of humor—"To deal with the highs and lows of living in another culture."

Hobbies & Interests

Outdoor pursuits: climbing, paddling, camping, mountain biking, and so on; reading, knitting, road cycling, improv comedy, writing, and spending time with family.

> *Biodynamic farming* is an alternative way of farming using "the cycle of the moons and the earth's own healing powers to enhance the productivity of the soil."

---

*Beth is in the process of starting an import/export company. She will sell arts and crafts in the United States from indigenous African cultures, mostly made by women, and plans to "cut out the middle man so the women receive their rightful share." "For some, when she sells an item, it means her kids will be able to eat. I enjoy work that has a mission to it."

Beth Llewelyn

Public Relations for Nintendo

> *"There's no greater thrill than seeing a story you've pitched appear in a print outlet or on TV, or hear people talking about it."*

Job Description

Beth works in public relations (PR) for video-game company Nintendo, where her main focus is to promote her company's products. She uses publicity promotions and media relationships to get product and company information to potential consumers. When asked the difference between public relations and marketing, Beth explains that although public relations is part of marketing, PR is looking for "in simple terms, free ink"—for example, the front-cover story of a magazine.

A Day on the Job

Acts as a spokesperson for her company. For example, she does media interviews, "getting on the phone with a reporter from a national newspaper talking about Nintendo DS, which is our new video-game system we recently launched, and why it's going to be a 'must-have' item for the holidays." • Plans and executes media tours throughout the country, where she meets with media to inform them about new products. • Plans and executes events to grab the media's attention. These events are usually big launch parties or press conferences. "For example, we'll host a celebrity event in Los Angeles. We invite young celebrities who are popular among our target demographic to a launch party. They get to play games first and we get media coverage from it." • Plans and attends trade shows. "At our industry's annual event called E3 (Electronic Entertainment Expo), we have a booth the size of a football field filled with game-play stations. PR is a big component of the show because we typically make big announcements or unveil new products." • Discusses strategy with an outside public relations agency that also promotes Nintendo. • Communicates with Nintendo's parent company in Japan, coordinating global communication tasks such as announcements and strategy. • Works with industry and financial analysts. • Participates in industry associations. • Manages other employees in her department. • Beth's department is also responsible for internal communications.

Job Likes

"There's no greater thrill than seeing a story you pitched appear in a print outlet or on TV, or hear people talking about it." • "It is very fast paced. No day is the same… it's difficult to get bored." • "I like the area of PR, and I like marketing. You can be a little bit more creative. We can do things a little more nontraditionally, which makes it fun." • "I work with some great people, which I think is very important in whatever job you have because you spend a lot of time with these people." • "I have a great company. I believe in their products."

Job Challenges

"It can get stressful… deadlines, sometimes just feeling like you can never get everything done." • It can be frustrating to plan a promotion and have a big news story break that overshadows the promotion. "And then you quickly have to figure out, okay how can we salvage this? What are other activities we can do to get our message across?"

Steps to Current Job

- Duke University in Durham, North Carolina; Bachelor of Arts in Economics.
- Worked in special events in Washington, D.C., for two years, which entailed working for political functions.
- Public relations for The Children's Museum in Washington, D.C., for approximately two years.
- *Freelance* public relations for the World Series of Poker while looking for a job in Los Angeles.
- Entertainment public relations in Los Angeles for approximately two years.
- Corporate public relations for three years.
- Public relations for Nintendo for nine years, where she is currently the Senior Director of Corporate Communications.

Advice

"Getting an education is very important," but Beth does not think that having a degree in PR is absolutely necessary. She says that you should take some classes in journalism and marketing. "Writing skills are critical." She also strongly recommends getting hands-on experience through summer jobs, internships, and volunteering.

For any career, Beth thinks that having a mentor to turn to for advice is beneficial. "If you have a dream, just go for it. Don't feel like because you're a girl you can't do that."

Helpful Personality Traits

Ability to multitask, motivated, self starter, confident, well-spoken, and flexible.

Hobbies & Interests

Travel, all forms of entertainment (movies, music, and books), biking, cooking, tennis, and jewelry making.

A *freelancer* works for herself, but provides work or expertise to different companies. Sometimes she works on a long-term assignment with one company, or she could have several smaller jobs with different companies.

Beth Satterfield

Web Strategist

"It really plays to my strengths because information architecture is also something you have to do as a journalist."

Web strategist Beth Satterfield gives a training session.

Job Description

Beth works for a *business intelligence software* company called SAS Institute, Inc., where she manages Web projects that support its numerous internal and external Web sites.

A Day on the Job

Starts the day by checking e-mails and making a "to-do" list. • Works on various projects throughout the day, either completing tasks herself or managing team members. • Manages the flow of information and ensures that information is found in the appropriate section on the Web site. The industry name for this is "information architecture." • Works with graphic designers to create the look of a Web site. • Writes and edits text for the sites. • Writes and makes adjustments to the HTML code for Web sites designed by graphic designers. • Keeps site information updated. Beth is responsible for keeping thousands of pages up-to-date. • Performs tests to ensure that the sites work properly. "Once the site is populated with content, then we run some testing with users to see if it is indeed usable. Does it make sense from the user's perspective?" • Extracts and provides Web analysis information. • Trains employees in other SAS departments and creates support materials for training purposes. • Provides support for international SAS Web sites.

Job Likes

"I love the people that I work with." • "I love the company that I work for, and I love the environment that I work in." SAS has always ranked highly on *Fortune* magazine's "100 Best Companies to Work For in America." The SAS campus offers many fringe benefits, including running trails, pool, gym, and on-site day care. • "I'm not stressed out because I don't have a job where if my thing doesn't get done, the whole world is going to fall apart. I've known for a very long time that I do not like that kind of pressure." This isn't to say that Beth doesn't find her job important. She just keeps things in perspective. • "It really plays to my strengths because information architecture is also something you have to do as a journalist. It's about organizing information, and you have to do that to write." • Beth likes that her job allows her to think objectively. "I like to think I have the ability to think outside-in, instead of inside-out. A lot of people get stuck in the information and forget how someone new coming to it might not see it or approach it the same way they would."

Job Challenges

"Graphic design is very subjective." Whether someone likes a design is all in the eye of the beholder. Designers might not always agree with Beth when she requests a change to their work. • In any company, there are always politics. "I like things based on good decisions rather than politics."

Steps to Current Job
- The University of North Carolina at Chapel Hill, Bachelor of Arts with a double major in Journalism and English.
- Special events planning internship for nine months.
- Public relations internship for six months.
- Director of Public Relations and Alumni Affairs for the UNC School of Nursing for two and a half years.
- Took classes toward a master's degree at UNC-Chapel Hill in Communications Research, concentrating in electronic communication and new media. Beth finished all but the thesis. During this time, Beth interned for SAS Institute, Inc.
- Worked in the corporate communications/Web department for SAS Institute, Inc., for six years.
- Part-time Web strategist. After having children, Beth scaled back her hours and currently works 24 hours a week.

Advice
Beth says that strong writing skills are a must. "If you can write, you learn how to think and present information in an organized fashion." She found her journalism degree to be a great foundation. Computer science and graphic design classes are also beneficial for a Web-based career.

"I think you have to know yourself really well to pick your career." It's important to think about what makes you happy. "It's not about money, because I do think the money will come if you're happy and do your job well." She adds that it is important to "do your job well no matter what it is. If you agree to work, you need to do a great job at whatever that is."

Helpful Personality Traits
Embraces new experiences, excited by learning, team player, and diplomatic.

Hobbies & Interests
Triathlons, running, reading, writing, soccer, and raising her children.

> *Business intelligence software:* "It's basically all of the information that businesses and organizations collect about themselves and their customers. We help them analyze that data."

Betty Webb

Director of International Studies and Professor of English

{ *"I am lucky I guess because the hardest work I do is also my favorite—traveling with students."* }

Betty Webb, Director of International Studies and college English professor, takes a break during a journey to Ecuador.

Job Description

Betty works with students and faculty coordinating their involvement in study-abroad programs and international faculty exchanges. "I spend about four and a half months out of the country, all but one of them leading or visiting students; and that suits me to a tee. At Christmas, I go somewhere I have not been before, but those trips have often become a starting point for some future opportunity for a Meredith student's travels." Betty was in Sri Lanka when the devastating tsunami hit. Fortunately, she was in another part of the country, but the next spring, she took a group of students to witness the devastation she escaped. Here, they got a first-hand account of how this natural disaster is affecting real people. They came back with their stories and photographs, ready to share what they learned and to start a tsunami-relief fund on their campus.

A Day on the Job

Meets with students and faculty and discusses their plans for involvement in the study-abroad program—answers any questions they might have. • Arranges accommodations, excursions, mobile phones—any detail necessary for a student's study-abroad program or a professor's exchange program. • Checks and responds to approximately 75 e-mails per day. • Teaches one English class per day. • Attends committee meetings. • Grades tests and papers. • Travels with students or visits students participating in study-abroad programs.

Job Likes

"I most like traveling with students, ensuring that they have interesting learning opportunities wherever we are—Italy or France or Sri Lanka. Almost anywhere in the world, really, can be the setting for life-changing, learning experiences for students."

Job Challenges

"I dislike the number of committee meetings I have. They interrupt the day and make it hard for me to be productive. Sometimes they seem like a waste of time."

Steps to Current Job

- Meredith College in Raleigh, North Carolina, Bachelor of Arts in English and history.
- High school English teacher for one and a half years.
- North Carolina State University in Raleigh, Master of Arts in English.
- College English teacher for four years while working on her doctorate.
- University of North Carolina at Chapel Hill, Doctorate in English.
- English Department Chair at Meredith College for seven years.
- Director of International Studies and English Professor at Meredith College.

Advice

Betty says that if you're interested in getting a position like hers, "You will need to go to college, and while you are there, you should study abroad at least once and work to master another language and culture." She also suggests working in the study-abroad office on your college campus to strengthen your international skill base. Once you have your undergraduate degree, Betty says, "You should go to graduate school for at least a master's degree—in international studies or some particular area studies, ideally. You should keep your language skills going in at least one language. That shows that you are serious about helping students have cross-cultural experiences."

It's no surprise that Betty thinks that you should learn to travel as soon as possible. "Australian women never know that women are not expected to be able to travel alone, and they do it brilliantly. I have run into them everywhere, happy by themselves and doing really interesting and adventurous things—hiking in the Anapurna Valley in Nepal, taking a canoe trip down the Zambezi in Zimbabwe, or trekking in Laos."

Helpful Personality Traits

Be detail oriented and organized. Betty also says, "Have a genuine curiosity about the world, a keen desire to see as much of it as possible, and transfer that desire to others. One needs to be a teacher because teaching students to be world citizens is not unlike teaching them to write an essay or to understand a play."

Hobbies & Interests

Travel, reading about the countries where she is traveling (biographies, histories, autobiographies, journalistic accounts, novels, short stories, and poems). "It is the way to understand a country, to get inside the culture you are visiting."

Beverly D. Setzer

School Principal

"I like setting up a school so that it is the best that it can be for the teachers to teach these children."

Job Description

Beverly is the principal for an elementary school, where she is responsible for managing every aspect of the school. Her job not only includes the obvious responsibility to the students; she also has many other responsibilities, including the entire school staff (teachers, bus drivers, janitors, and so on), the budget, professional development for the teachers, and being a liaison between parents and teachers and also between her school and the county. "What I always tell parents is my number-one responsibility is to ensure the safety of their children… and then number two, ensure that they [the children] get a quality education."

A Day on the Job

Starts the day by making coffee for the staff and checking e-mails. • Greets the staff, children, and parents as they arrive. "That just makes me visible and accessible. There is always interaction, problem-solving." • Monitors the children to make sure they get to their classrooms safely. • Walks the halls to make sure that classes are settled. • Returns to her office for appointments, to deal with discipline issues, and to return phone calls. Other responsibilities may include observing classrooms, attending school-related meetings outside of the school, managing the school money, and staff-enrichment training. • Attends lunch. "I think being visible for the kids is very important. They need to know that I'm here." • Continues tasks she started that morning. • Checks with the bus drivers before children are let out of school. • Helps load buses and is visible to the parents. "The hardest time for children to behave is unsupervised time." • Returns phone calls, usually from parents. • Checks on after-school programs. • Waits for buses to return and checks with their drivers. • Leaves anywhere between 4:30 p.m. and 7:00 p.m., depending on her schedule.

Job Likes
"Every day is different, and that is actually one of the things that I really like about this job. Rarely can I plan my day. I like change. I like variety." • "I love the children. I always wanted to be an elementary school teacher." • "When you are doing what you are supposed to be doing, you know it. I really do feel like I'm in my niche. I am the most gratified, and I feel the most comfortable in this position." • "I like providing for the teachers. I like supporting the teachers. I try to keep the teachers built up and professional." • "I like setting up a school so that it is the best that it can be for the teachers to teach these children."

Job Challenges
"I can't even say that I don't like the paperwork."

Steps to Current Job
- Western Carolina University in Cullowhee, North Carolina, Bachelor of Science in Early Childhood Education and Master of Arts in Early Childhood Education with a concentration in reading.
- Reading teacher for five and a half years.
- Staff for North Carolina Representative in the U.S. House of Representatives in Washington, D.C., for two years. During her time in the D.C. area, she earned 50 additional hours of college credit in math and gifted education classes from The University of Virginia, Virginia Tech, and Northern Virginia Community College.
- Elementary classroom teacher for three years.
- Elementary reading specialist for five years.
- Middle school reading specialist for one year.
- Georgia State University in Atlanta, Educational Specialist degree in School Administration and Supervision.
- Middle school assistant principal for five years.
- Middle school math teacher for one year.
- Elementary school principal for five years.

Advice

Beverly says to find what you are passionate about in education and start there. "Learning did not come easy to me as a child, but I had a teacher who believed in me. I became a reading specialist because I understood the negative impact that having a learning issue can have on a person. It makes you feel dumb when you are not necessarily at all." On the road to becoming a principal, "excel as a teacher," and as a teacher, put yourself in positions of leadership. Beverly has also found that the more instructional background someone has, the better principal he or she makes.

"Women need to decide what's important to them and follow that, but they need to have passion for what they're doing. If you don't have a passion for it, don't do it. Find out what your passion is first, because you're going to be doing it for a while. It needs to matter."

Helpful Personality Traits

Good judgment, leader, people person, good communication skills, personal integrity, able to handle conflict, able to make well-thought-out decisions and can handle not being liked. "When I go home at the end of the day, it matters to me that I'm respected because it can't matter to me that I'm liked."

Hobbies & Interests

Knitting, golf, reading, and cooking.

"Destiny is not a matter of chance, it is a matter of choice. It is not a thing to be waited for, it is a thing to be achieved."

—William Jennings Bryan

Carol Boyers Givens

Museum Objects Conservator

{ *"I always wanted to mix science, history, and art together."* }

Job Description

A museum objects conservator preserves and stabilizes museum objects that are in need of care. "To conserve means to preserve for posterity and to preserve and restore the integrity of an object." Carol points out that this is not object restoration when an object is brought back to its original condition. Rather, in conservation, an object is stabilized so it will not deteriorate further. Carol works as an independent consultant for museums.

A Day on the Job

Researches the history of an object in need of care. • Writes a detailed treatment report discussing the description and the condition of the object. • Photographs the object. • Performs conservation treatments to various museum objects. "Right now, I'm working on two Plains Indian pieces. One is a cradle board cover that's covered in beads, and another is a saddle blanket that is also covered in an enormous amount of beadwork." She is stitching the beading back on these objects using the same stitching methods used by the Plains Indians. Carol follows conservation ethics, where every treatment she uses is reversible. • Gives conservation lectures to museum staff and to fellow conservators. • Keeps up with the business aspects required of owning her own business.

Job Likes

"I have to tax my brain everyday to try to come up with a different treatment, and that's kind of fun." • She likes the variety in her work. Carol works with many types of objects compared to someone who specializes in just one medium. For example, a paintings conservator works strictly with paintings. • Working as a consultant allows her the flexibility to decide how much and when she wants to work. This is helpful while raising her children. "You can pick and choose your hours." • "I love thinking about the history behind an object." Right now, Carol's imagination is working overtime as she works with some of President James Monroe's belongings. • "I like the thought that I'm helping my children, the next generation, and their grandchildren see these things for a lifetime. It's all about preserving history."

Job Challenges

"In order to treat these objects, it involves a lot of solvent usage. I'll end up wearing a respirator mask all day. It just gets really old." • Having to tend to the necessary, business aspects of owning a business is not Carol's favorite part of her job. "It takes quite a long time when you own your own business to do the taxes. They get complex and cumbersome."

Steps to Current Job

- The University of Virginia in Charlottesville, Bachelor of Arts in Anthropology and Archeology.

- Archeologist for four years. "I loved going on excavations. I kept coming up with all of these artifacts coming out of the ground and thinking 'Oh my gosh, what happens to them now? They're going to totally fall apart if somebody doesn't take care of them.'"
- Museum curator for four years.
- Virginia Commonwealth University in Richmond, VA, studies in Chemistry.
- Museum objects conservator apprenticeship for eight years.
- Museum objects conservator.

Advice
"You need to go and try to volunteer for curators and conservators at museums to see if that's exactly what you want to do." If you like history, chemistry, and art, conservation is a good field to apply them all.

"Don't give up and keep working towards your goals."

Helpful Personality Traits
Patient; enjoys the outdoors; respectful of art and enjoys science, history, and art.

Hobbies & Interests
Camping, hiking, biking, canoeing, and being outdoors.

Caroline Palmer

Ballet Choreologist

{ *"I love traveling around the world, meeting dancers from different countries."* }

Job Description
Caroline documents the choreography of a ballet using a special notation. "It is precise recording of the movements intended by a choreographer—a sort of exact documentation of his or her wishes and designs. My task is to notate all the steps in the context of the music, the space, and also the other dancers on the stage."* To better explain her job, she compares it to writing music notes.

---

*Taken from an article by Helena Bartlova in the May 2004 issue of *Národní Divadlo* (National Theatre) *Magazine of Prague.*

A Day on the Job
Watches dance rehearsals in a studio and takes notes about the choreography. • Assists the choreographer in teaching a ballet to the ballet company. • Attends the first performance of a ballet. Caroline compares her notes to the final choreography in the ballet and updates her notation. The final notation is filed and stored for copyright purposes.

Job Likes
"I love traveling around the world, meeting dancers from different countries." Caroline is based in London, England. She just completed a job in Prague, the capital of the Czech Republic. Her next job is in Atlanta, Georgia, USA. • Caroline enjoys working with her choreographer because she finds him "very talented, very funny, and always happy." • Her job allows her to work in the theatre, which she missed while working as a dance teacher.

Job Challenges
"It is a bit scary going into a studio full of 60 dancers, who may not speak English, and teaching them a new ballet." (Caroline speaks English and German.)

Steps to Current Job
- Studied classical dance technique in London, England.
- Classical dancer for 10 years.
- Classical dance technique instructor for 17 years.
- Completed the choreologist course at the Benesh Institute in London, England.
- Choreologist. Caroline's projects as a choreologist include work with the London City Ballet, the Royal Swedish Ballet, the English National Ballet, and working for the choreographer Christopher Hampson.

Advice
Caroline advises people interested in her career to have a dance background and to learn to read music. She feels that her background in dance and as a dance instructor helps her to better understand the dancers and the choreographer, and also helps her as a choreologist. "When I look back, I am immensely satisfied that my professional journey took me through dancing to teaching because now I can build on those things in choreology. Without those valuable experiences, I would never understand how a dancer feels."*

*Taken from an article by Helena Bartlova in the May 2004 issue of *Národní Divadlo* (National Theatre) *Magazine of Prague.*

Her advice to young women is to "Do what you really want to do, even if it doesn't pay very well. It's better to be happy and fulfilled than rich!"

Helpful Personality Traits
Patient ("It takes 12 hours to write 30 seconds of movement!") and confident.

Hobbies & Interests
Reading, walking, and traveling.

Cathy Jenkins Wilson

Advertising Broadcast Producer

{ *"What people hate about it, oftentimes is what people love about it."* }

Cathy Jenkins Wilson, advertising broadcast producer, supervises an edit session.

Job Description
Cathy works as an advertising producer for a national advertising agency and produces radio and television commercials (a.k.a. "spots") from start to finish.

This includes pre-production—where the spot is organized and planned—shooting the spot, and then editing it. Her main goal is to make sure that the ideas of the creative team (the writer and art director) are carried out within the allotted budget.

A Day on the Job
Makes schedules that outline when shoots, edit sessions, and the delivery of the spot(s) to television and radio stations will occur. • Estimates and negotiates costs of shooting, travel, editing, music, and talent. • Researches vendors and determines with her writer and art director which ones to hire—"...anyone from the director, the editor, the music company." • Researches legal issues—for example, music licensing. • Travels to shoots and edit sessions. • Mediates communication between *account services team* and creative team—"Usually the tension between creatively what you want, how much you can afford, and how much time you have to get it done, is what creates the pressure cooker of advertising. I'm like the den mother."

Job Likes
"I love that each project is different." • "I love that I'm always working with a different group of people. I'm exposed to people from all walks of life." • A typical television production can last as long as three months. That allows Cathy to really get to know the people working on the job. "It's almost like college when you were in the dorm together. You're sleeping [at the same hotel] and eating together." • Cathy likes that she has traveled all over the country and abroad for her job.

Job Challenges
"Creativity is such a subjective thing. Everybody thinks that they're right," and Cathy can't argue that it's "good" or "bad" when she doesn't agree with a concept. It creates a lot of frustration and tension. • "The other thing that I really hate about advertising, which you find with any kind of creative business, is trends; because there is a wanting to be fresh and inventive and new and hot all the time, but what I hear a lot are people just following other trends." • Cathy travels a lot for her job and says, "It's wonderful, and it is hard. It's funny because I love it, but I love it in spurts; but it never works that way. Where I get tired is if it's this long, straight run."

Steps to Current Job
- University of North Carolina at Chapel Hill, Bachelor of Arts with a double major in Speech Communications and Radio, Television, and Motion Picture.
- Public Television producer for two years.

- Advertising production coordinator for three years.
- Advertising producer.

Advice

Cathy thinks that the best way to get your foot in the door in this field is to find an internship, and this will also help you decide whether advertising is right for you. She says, "the wonderful thing about doing internships is they help you figure out what you want to be." And, they're a great way to earn some extra cash. As Cathy recalls, "When you're in college, you're poor. You want to try and get paid or get credit out of it. I just think that an internship is a great way to get in."

"Don't feel the need to be apologetic for being a woman." Cathy says that when you first start your career, "There's that weird balance of being confident, smart, and aggressive." She says that you can be a woman and feminine and still be successful.

Helpful Personality Traits

Creative, adventurous, good people skills, analytical, mathematically inclined, and a love of history—"A breadth of knowledge and interests is what feeds the best ads and helps them connect to realities."

Hobbies & Interests

Gardening, pottery, cooking, and connecting with people.

> *Account services team* is a group of people within an advertising agency assigned to manage the client's (the company paying for the advertising) needs and expectations.

Cecily Steppe

Marine Biologist

{ *"I love being on the water."* }

Job Description

"I study the way organisms interact with the ocean." Cecily works for the U.S. Naval Academy, where she splits her time between teaching biological oceanography to college students and conducting research. Her current area of research has to do with the effects of winds and currents on the survival of baby fish and crabs.

A Day on the Job

Teaches two oceanography classes to the students at the Naval Academy. • Conducts research either in the laboratory or at the ocean. Much of her summer is spent at the ocean collecting data. The other months of the year, she is conducting laboratory-based experiments and analyzing data. • Attends to the usual teaching duties such as grading papers, deciding on course materials, planning classes, and creating class syllabi. • Writes articles about her research to be published in journals or to be presented at national and international oceanography meetings. • Applies for grants to obtain funding for her research and salary.

Job Likes

"I love being on the water." Cecily says that she has known since she was five that she wanted to be near the water and work as a marine biologist. • "I really enjoy the research component; it's very gratifying." • Cecily also enjoys teaching her classes because she enjoys the interaction with "really great students." • Attending national and international oceanography meetings, Cecily likes that she is continually learning.

Job Challenges

There is a lot of administrative paperwork in Cecily's job, and she doesn't find it very fulfilling. • Writing grants is time consuming, and it takes Cecily away from doing research.

Steps to Current Job

- Yale University in New Haven, Connecticut; Bachelor of Science in Biology; member of the sailing team.
- University of Delaware in Lewes, Delaware; Ph.D. in Oceanography.
- Post-Doctoral Fellowship at the NOAA National Marine Fisheries in Beaufort, North Carolina, for one year.
- Assistant Professor at the United States Naval Academy in Annapolis, Maryland.

Advice

Cecily suggests pursuing "an undergraduate degree in one of the basic sciences," such as biology or chemistry, because she feels that it is important to have a "fundamental knowledge" of the basic sciences before continuing with your master's and Ph.D., and it is easier to take basic science classes when you are still an undergraduate. She also points out that you can work as a marine biologist with just a bachelor's degree, but having a master's degree allows you more job versatility. As you progress into the Ph.D. level, you become more specific in your field of study and work.

"Do something you love because whatever you decide to do, there are going to be aspects that are really hard, but if you really like the topic, you'll be able to get through it."

Helpful Personality Traits
Self-motivator, team player, and dedicated.

Hobbies & Interests
Swimming, sailing, triathlons, and outdoor activities.

GET THAT DEGREE BEFORE STARTING A FAMILY!

It is definitely easier to earn a degree when you have only yourself to think about. Once you have the responsibilities that come with a house, a husband, and children, time for yourself is difficult to find.

It is not impossible to earn a degree when you have a family, but it certainly is more difficult.

Charlotte Michie

Licensed Clinical Social Worker (LCSW)

"I love the flexibility. I love the autonomy. No one tells me what to do."

Job Description
"I assist people in making changes in their lives—ideally to change their belief systems." Charlotte uses a variety of therapeutic techniques to help individuals do this, such as *hypnotherapy, energy psychotherapy,* and "plain old *psychotherapy.*" She also works with groups, using *Dialectical Behavior Therapy (DBT)* to teach people how to become "unstuck in their world of black and white."

A Day on the Job

Sees three to four individuals (one per session) a day—Charlotte explains that she is in the office only three days a week, but says, "Sometimes my days are 12 hours long, where I see someone at nine in the morning, and I see my last person at 8:30 at night. I typically only take Sundays off. Believe it or not. Even though I only see clients three days a week." When Charlotte isn't in sessions, she's doing many of the activities in the rest of this list. • Prepares for DBT sessions by printing sections of the manual she has developed. • Conducts one group session per day. "I always do a group. So, I have one group a day that I typically see from 5:30 [p.m.] to 7:00 [p.m.]; and that's anywhere from six to eight people. I run the group by myself." • Writes notes (suggestions) for individual clients' charts. • Reads and formulates new ideas for clients. "I do think a lot about my cases. How can I give them the piece of the puzzle that's missing?" • Creates "homework" and handouts for her clients. Charlotte thinks that it is really important to "keep the session alive between now and the next time I see you [the patient]." • Attends conferences and workshops to increase her skills set.

Job Likes

Charlotte's job allows her to be very creative. "Every person that walks in... I have no idea what they're going to bring. It's part detective work." • "I love the flexibility. I love the autonomy. No one tells me what to do." • Because she is impacted by her clients' problems, Charlotte is very self-aware and is able to work on her own personal issues. • Charlotte says that it's really rewarding to see her patients "bloom."

Job Challenges

"Any kind of administrative work is low on my totem pole." • Charlotte says that she's gotten better at it, but marketing herself is difficult.

Steps to Current Job
- North Carolina State University in Raleigh, Bachelor of Science and Master of Science in Psychology.
- Management organization development specialist for 18 months.
- Part owner in a software development company for 10 years.
- East Carolina University in Greenville, North Carolina; Master of Science in Social Psychology and Social Work.
- Internships necessary to earn license in social work for three years (3,000 hours of work required).
- Private-practice, Licensed Clinical Social Worker for four years.

Advice

Charlotte recommends taking a self test, such as Myers-Briggs, and find out "who you are from a behaviorist point of view." Make sure that your personality is a good match for being a therapist. She says, "If you don't know who you are, you're not going to be successful in this business." Charlotte thinks that it's important to talk to people in this field. Ask them what they like and what they don't like about their jobs. Then ask the person whom you feel most comfortable with if you can shadow him or her for a day or a week. Some clients would allow you to sit in on a session, but the therapist would have to clear that first.

"I think that it's really important to have mentors. If there's a person out there that you really connect with, be willing to venture out and ask them for support. They don't have to be in the field that you want to go into. Everybody needs sounding boards."

Charlotte also thinks that dreams are key. "It is so important to know that you've got a dream and that you're willing to follow it."

Helpful Personality Traits

Introspective, intuitive, flexible, above-average IQ, good with analogies and metaphors, highly imaginative and able to imagine the best for people.

Hobbies & Interests

Gardening, reading, stained-glass work, writing, and meditating.

Hypnotherapy facilitates access to a client's subconscious mind, in order to uncover and explore memories, emotions, and past events that might affect a person's conscious mind. It can be used to help treat behavioral problems and phobias.

Psychotherapy is "talk therapy," or working through problems by talking with a trained individual. It also includes learning life skills and how to implement them.

Energy psychotherapy is also called *power therapy* and addresses the effects of bioenergy systems (subtle energy generated by people) on human emotion and behavior.

Dialectical behavioral therapy is a cognitive-behavioral approach that teaches people how to become "unstuck in their world of black and white" through dialogue and relationship.

Charlotte Thomas Riddle

Pediatrician

{ *"The next day they come in and they're all smiles. That's very reward-ing."* }

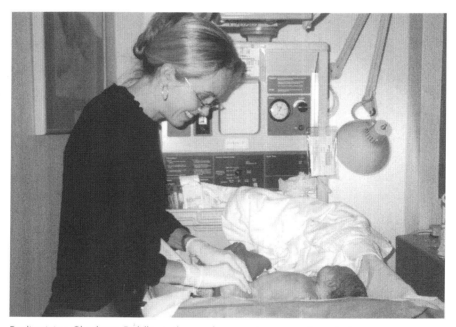

Pediatrician Charlotte Riddle smiles as she examines a newborn baby.
Courtesy Claire Moss.

Job Description

Charlotte provides medical care for children from birth to approximately 20 years.

A Day on the Job

Starts her day by making rounds at the hospital. She is present at scheduled *cae-sarean sections*, *circumcises* newborn boys, and checks on newborn babies and sick children admitted to the hospital. Each doctor in Charlotte's practice takes a turn doing hospital duty. • In her office, she examines check-up patients and sick children. "We have a check-up or two on the hour, with four or five sick visits. Each doctor sets their own schedule." • Documents patient information on each patient she treats. • Acts as a consultant for health-department nurses and family physicians. • Returns to the hospital to check on newborns and admitted patients. "We see any new babies that might have been born that day and then we go on rounds to see our other patients." • When she is on night call, Charlotte sees patients and takes emergency calls throughout the night. Evening shifts also rotate among doctors.

Job Likes

"You're heart to heart with the parents." Charlotte enjoys the interaction with children and their parents. • Charlotte job-shares with another pediatrician, which means she and her partner split the responsibilities of one doctor. This allows both of them to work part-time (about 30 hours a week each) while raising their families. • She finds her job very rewarding. "You give them [the patient] the right medicine; the next day they come in and they're all smiles. That's very rewarding." She also feels that she is making "a difference in their [the patients' and their families'] lives, and you also are feeding yourself." • Pediatrics is never boring; there is always variety. • "I like my partners a lot. I love to have people that I can talk to on a different level about different things. And to have that camaraderie really helps in the day-to-day." • "I love to pore through my journals and learn about new things, and there is always something new to learn."

Job Challenges

"I find it challenging to balance the stressful job involving critical care of children and the stressful job of raising a family. In today's society, this is a challenge for both men and women, fathers and mothers." • "I like my sleep," and Charlotte's schedule can deprive her of it. "Pediatrics involves long hours and hard work." • Sometimes in today's society, people tend to "place blame" and "point fingers." It is challenging as a doctor to handle that stress. • "When you put your heart and your soul into something, you become vulnerable to people."

Steps to Current Job
- University of the South, Sewanee, Tennessee; Bachelor of Arts in Religion.
- University of South Carolina in Columbia; the first two years of medical school.
- Medical University of South Carolina in Charleston, South Carolina; third and fourth years of medical school, Medical Doctor degree, honor society.
- University of Virginia in Charlottesville; Pediatric residency for three years.
- Pediatrician in a pediatric office and currently president of that practice.

Advice

If you are interested in pediatrics, you need to get some clinical experience. Charlotte suggests working in your local emergency room or volunteering/ interning at a pediatric office. She points out that medical schools don't require you to attend the most elite undergraduate school, but they do require a good grade-point average. So keep your grades up. Charlotte also adds that it's important to "keep your options open."

"If you respect your mind and body, the rest comes more easily. You become more disciplined, you feel better about yourself, and your moods are better when you respect your body. Respect your mind by constantly challenging yourself. Read and keep your avenues open." Charlotte recommends having a role model or mentor because "women need not reinvent the wheel." Her other bit of advice to young women is "before you get your family started, have that degree in your back pocket... because having a family is so much more consuming than I ever imagined."

Helpful Personality Traits

Intrigued with science, inquisitive, a good listener, empathetic, and must relate to all levels of society.

Hobbies & Interests

Music (piano, guitar, and flute), reading, creative projects with her children, hiking, camping, gardening, and exploring her spirituality.

> *Caesarean section* is a surgery performed on a pregnant woman where an incision is made in the abdominal wall and uterus to remove a baby.
>
> *Circumcision* is removing the fold of skin covering the tip of the penis.

Claire Moss

Pediatric Occupational Therapist

"I wanted to do something that was helping people in their lives in a more tender way."

Job Description

A pediatric occupational therapist works with children, through age-appropriate play, to develop their daily living skills. The children are disabled, delayed (not reaching developmental milestones), or have been in accidents. *Occupational therapy* (OT) is similar to *physical therapy,* but in occupational therapy the goal is working on completing specific tasks through activities of daily living. For small children, daily living skills might include tasks such as latching on while nursing or taking a bottle, holding a bottle, pulling up, rolling over, or having the desire to shake a rattle. For older children, daily living skills might include tasks such as walking (perhaps with a walker), writing, turning a door knob, or feeding themselves.

A Day on the Job

Reviews files of the children she plans to visit and determines each child's goals. • Gathers supplies for her appointments with the children. "I decide what equipment I need and what are some toys that are good motivators." • Visits children in their homes, approximately four appointments a day. • Meets monthly with a team of caregivers. The team consists of Claire, a physical therapist, a speech therapist, and a developmental therapist. "We would review the child's goals, review their progress, make adaptations as we need it."

Job Likes

"I love the flexibility of it." There are many reasons that OT is flexible. First, "you can move anywhere and do it." The hours are flexible, which Claire points out is helpful when you have a family. And, there is flexibility within the career because there are many different specializations, such as hand, brain injury, geriatric, and school system. There are also opportunities to work as a traveling OT. • "I wanted to do something that was helping people in their lives in a more tender way." Claire sees her patients reach milestones and she also gets to share in the excitement of families witnessing that. "You see these parents and how excited they are for their child to be able to walk or do something they could not do before." • There is a lot of job security because there will always be a need for OTs, especially with the expanding older population. • "It's a steady, secure income."

Job Challenges

Health-care issues are frustrating when the patient's health-care provider does not agree with or will not pay for the OT's recommended treatment. "You see a patient that really needs something and their health care won't cover it." • "The emotional part is draining." Claire often works with disabled children, children who have been in accidents, and children who are "losing a function in their life and all of the other family members are watching them lose that function."

Steps to Current Job

- University of Southern California in Los Angeles, Bachelor of Science in Occupational Therapy.
- Completed required internship at two hospitals (six months).
- Occupational therapist for a children's therapy center for one year.
- Occupational therapist for a school system for two years.
- Occupational therapist for a state early-intervention program and school system for four years.
- Currently a full-time mom, part-time photographer, and part-time OT.

Advice

Claire says that it would be helpful to attend a college that offers both an under-graduate and graduate degree in OT because you can begin to earn credit for your master's while you are an undergraduate.

"I think that it is important if you are planning on having children and if you know you want a family, to choose something that is flexible and that offers a lot of variety within the career." She recommends that you "find something that taps into all the different sides of yourself, like your creative side, your intellectual side, your social side." Also remember, "don't be afraid to change your career if you don't like it. It's never too late."

Helpful Personality Traits

Compassionate, patient, and enjoys health sciences.

Hobbies & Interests

Photography, home renovation, hiking, and pottery.

Occupational therapy "helps people improve their ability to perform tasks in their daily living and working environments. They [occupational therapists] work with individuals who have conditions that are mentally, physically, developmentally, or emotionally disabling. They also help them to develop, recover, or maintain daily living and work skills. Occupational therapists help clients not only to improve their basic motor functions and reasoning abilities, but also to compensate for permanent loss of function. Their goal is to help clients have independent, productive, and satisfying lives.*"

Physical therapy "helps restore function, improve mobility, relieve pain, and prevent or limit permanent physical disabilities of patients suffering from injuries or disease. They [physical therapists] restore, maintain, and promote overall fitness and health. Their patients include accident victims and individuals with disabling conditions such as low-back pain, arthritis, heart disease, fractures, head injuries, and cerebral palsy.*" See also the profile for Theresa Wagoner on page 224.

---

*U.S. Department of Labor, Bureau of Labor Statistics, Occupational Outlook Handbook, www.bls.gov/oco/home.htm.

Claudia Brown

Architectural Survey Coordinator for the North Carolina State Historic Preservation Office

{ *"I like the intellectual aspect of this—the research, the evaluation aspect, being a sleuth."* }

Job Description

Claudia helps to make sure that there is a record of North Carolina's historic properties and encourages their preservation. She oversees a program that surveys (gathers information) on the state's historic properties. Municipalities and counties can apply to her office for grants that help fund these surveys. For every 40 cents a municipality raises, the state will match with 60 cents.

A Day on the Job

Reviews grant applications from cities and towns. • Helps local governments find consultants to perform the survey once grants are awarded. • Draws up contracts between cities and towns and consultants. • Oversees consultants' work. "They can't just send it in at the end of the project; and I review it as it comes in." Claudia also makes sure that the consultants (through their written entries and photographs) are correctly identifying the historical significance of buildings. • Edits survey write-ups so that they are ready for architectural-survey publications. "If the local governments take the next step of publishing survey results, the results should be ready to drop into a publication." • Oversees a region of the state for inquiries from private citizens and public officials regarding historic properties. "I get all kinds of inquiries. 'I have a historic property. What do I do?' And so, I'll tell them about our programs." • Goes on field visits to potential historic properties or to properties that are under survey. "If I can't make an opinion based on photos... I'll make a site visit and meet with the property owners... and find out what they know about it." • Speaks to groups about The State Historic Preservation Office's programs. • Works on special projects. "Right now, I'm working on an ongoing survey of *Rosenwald* schools.

Job Likes

"I like the variety." • "I like being able to get out "in the field," working with people, helping people." • "I spend a lot of the time in the office, but I'm not chained to my desk." • "I like the intellectual aspect of this work—the research, the evaluation, being a sleuth."

Job Challenges

"I'm in a big bureaucracy, and sometimes it's hard to get things done because you're part of it." • "Sometimes the politics can be pretty maddening… state legislators calling you up and demanding that you give a constituent what he wants, and we have to function within our programs' regulations and guidelines."

Steps to Current Job

- Wake Forest University, Winston-Salem, North Carolina; Bachelor of Arts in Spanish.
- Statistical typist for an accounting firm for two years.
- University of North Carolina at Chapel Hill; Master of Arts in Art History and completed Ph.D. coursework in Art History. Held part-time jobs, including secretarial work, acting as an assistant to the university's art museum registrar and as a teaching assistant.
- Historic preservation consultant for eight years.
- Worked for a pizza franchiser in operations and marketing and as administrative assistant to the president for two years.
- National register coordinator for the Kentucky Heritage Council for one year.
- Since 1989, Claudia has been with the North Carolina State Historical Preservation Office, where she has worked in numerous roles—from national register coordinator to branch supervisor. She is now the architectural survey coordinator.

Advice

Claudia says, "It's not easy to get into a state preservation office job because we require related experience. Intern with an established preservationist who is out doing field work." She also advises that you need to know buildings, so take architectural history courses. "Take as many of them as you can. Taking world architectural history isn't enough. You need to know *vernacular architecture*, not just the high styles." Lastly, Claudia says, "Learn to express yourself, both orally and in writing. It's really important to be able to communicate."

"If you have an interest in something, and it seems daunting, figure it out," says Claudia. A mentor can often help you do this, she explains. Claudia maintains close relationships with two of her early mentors and credits them with teaching her writing and business skills.

Helpful Personality Traits

Intellectual curiosity, diplomacy, liking people and having a good eye. "… train your eye to observe and be critical."

Hobbies & Interests

Reading novels and newspapers, knitting, viewing and collecting art, and public service. "I've served on city task forces, and I'm also a *guardian ad litem*."

Julius *Rosenwald* was a CEO of Sears Roebuck, whose fund distributed grants to build schools for African Americans in the early 20th century. Claudia explains, "He enabled over 5,000 schools for blacks to be built in the south, and North Carolina had more than any other state. We had over 800."

Vernacular architecture uses common regional forms, decorative motifs, and materials, usually designed by someone other than an architect. Vernacular architecture is often owner-built with local materials, using local building customs and techniques.

North Carolina's Guardian ad Litem's mission is to provide trained independent advocates to represent and promote the best interests of abused, neglected, and dependent children in the state court system and to work toward a plan that ensures that these children are in a safe permanent home. (For more information, see www.volunteermatch.org/results/org_detail.jsp?orgid=19354.)

Connie McNab

Children's Book Illustrator/Artist

{ *"I could never do a blah-looking book. I'm just really into color."* }

Children's book illustrator Connie McNab takes a break with Mortimer, a character from one of the books she illustrated.

Job Description

Connie draws illustrations for children's books that visually communicate a story or an idea. Sometimes the illustrations are used in conjunction with words and sometimes not.

A Day on the Job

Visualizes and thinks of ideas for drawings. "The thing that is really time-consuming is thinking up the illustrations." • Quickly sketches ideas, and then draws them more precisely. • Outlines drawings in black ink. • Paints finished drawings. "And the painting takes a long time because I use a lot of colors. It could take a week to do one page." • Travels to events to promote her book, *The Story of Mortimer Ant.* "I dress as the Mortimer character, and I read in this Mortimer voice when we're [Connie and her husband] doing our presentation."

Job Likes

"I feel like I'm a fairly creative person. I've always liked to draw. Even as a teacher, I always tried to incorporate art into just about everything we did." • "I love color. I could never do a blah-looking book. I'm just really into color." • Illustration is a creative field, and Connie enjoys coming up with work that is nontraditional. In The Story of Mortimer Ant, she gave Mortimer (an ant) shoes to wear. • "I love working on the computer." Because color is integral to her style, Connie enjoys experimenting with it on the computer and finding the color opportunities a computer allows.

Job Challenges

Although there isn't much about her job that Connie doesn't like, she says it can be time-consuming, which often causes a lot of frustration because she wants to see the finished product as quickly as possible.

Steps to Current Job

- University of Georgia, Athens; Bachelor of Science in Education.
- Valdosta State University, Georgia; Master of Arts in Reading.
- Middle school teacher for one year.
- High school teacher for one year.
- Elementary teacher for 20 years.
- Children's book illustrator/artist. Connie started illustrating professionally when her husband's children's book was accepted by a publisher.

Advice

Do something that really interests you. "The best scenario would be to find something that you love and get paid for it." Even if this isn't possible, Connie suggests that you find a career that incorporates your interests. For example, if you love art, but it won't pay the bills, try to find a career where you can apply this passion (for example, art buying).

Helpful Personality Traits
Patient, observant, creative, and an eye for color.

Hobbies & Interests
Gardening, reading, painting faux finishes for interiors, computer graphics, and interior design.

For more information, see www.mortimerandfriends.com.

Dale Scott

Director of Child Services for a Community Mental-Health Center

{ *"I'm amazed about the resiliency and strength of children to overcome difficulties."* }

Job Description
Dale is a Licensed Clinical Social Worker and her job has two main focuses: clinical consultant and administrator. When consulting with her staff and the community, she offers advice and reviews cases on children's mental-health issues. As administrator, she manages all of the employees, the day-to-day operations, and the services provided by her facility. "I specialize in working with and advocating for abused and neglected children and with children and adults who have experienced trauma."

A Day on the Job
Oversees the entire operations of her facility. Dale is responsible for managing a large staff of counselors and support staff. She also manages personnel issues, referrals, billing, medical records, and all other aspects related to properly running a mental-health center. "It's really like managing a doctor's office." • Supervises therapists in her practice to help them obtain their licensure. "For a therapist to be licensed, they have to have two years of weekly supervision to review their cases by a licensed supervisor." • Serves in the community on various boards and agencies that deal with children. "I'm an advocate for children's

mental-health issues. That means on these committees and boards, they look to me as an expert about mental health and the needs of children and families in our community. It also means that I will speak on behalf of those children and families who are impoverished and lack the resources to obtain psychiatric treatment. We don't turn anyone away." • Counsels clients when staff therapists are not available, or if the case is particularly complicated, and provides support to parents. • Writes grants and seeks contracts to get money to pay for services and to develop creative programming. • Troubleshoots mental-health concerns and problems in the community. "If there's a problem in the community regarding a child's mental-health needs, they call me."

Job Likes
"I like working directly with children and families and with other therapists to help people improve their quality of life." • "I like being able to have an influence in the community on behalf of children." • "I'm amazed about the resiliency and strength of children to overcome difficulties. It encourages me to feel hopeful and to continue my work with optimism."

Job Challenges
"Recently, in our political and economic climate, there have been state and federal cutbacks for psychiatric services for children, especially prevention services. In the long run, it is much more costly if we do not try to prevent problems. This is very frustrating for me to see children and families go without needed treatment."

Steps to Current Job
- Wesleyan College in Macon, Georgia; psychology and general college courses.
- University of Georgia at Athens, Bachelor of Science in Sociology.
- Mental health assistant for an adolescent psychiatric hospital for five years.
- University of South Carolina at Columbia; took classes toward a master's in social work.
- University of North Carolina at Chapel Hill; Master's in Social Work specializing in Mental Health.
- Interned at a community mental-health center. After completing the requirements to become a licensed social worker, Dale was promoted to therapist and was at the facility for four years, where she worked with children and adults and their families. She worked closely with the domestic-violence center and conducted a group for men who were batterers.
- Family therapist and clinical social worker at a psychiatric hospital for five years.
- Private-practice therapist in the evenings while working as a clinical social worker and therapist.

- Lead therapist at a community mental-health center, where she worked with mentally ill, homeless adults.
- Expert witness for court regarding child abuse and neglect.
- Community mental-health center." Dale started as the director of early intervention (working with special-needs children age zero to three and their families) and worked her way up to her present position as director.

Advice

While Dale was working toward her undergraduate degree, she volunteered as a swim coach for a blind school. "It was the first time I'd been around children with disabilities… so I think during that time I began to know that I wanted to work with kids with special needs." Dale says that it is important that you have a genuine interest in human behavior and to find out whether you enjoy working with children with emotional problems. You can do this by volunteering like she did, interning, or working in a group home. "Talk with other therapists and ask them questions." If you don't know a clinical social worker to talk with, ask your high school guidance counselor to help you find someone in your community. If you're in college, talk with the mental-health counselors on campus.

"There are always life circumstances that can interfere or detour the path you have chosen, so you have to persevere and be strong, and sometimes you're the only one that will encourage yourself." While Dale was working toward her master's, she went through two pregnancies and a back surgery. It took her seven years to earn her master's, but she hung in and accomplished her goal. "Watch the women who have gone before you, and learn from them. Then be someone that other women can learn from. Strive to make our world a better place."

Helpful Personality Traits

Kind, patient, a good listener, tolerant, accepting of diversity, and interested in human development and relationships.

Hobbies & Interests

Reading, gardening, camping, music, spending time with friends, working as a hospital chaplain, and leading interdenominational religious retreats.

"Success is often achieved by those who don't know that failure is inevitable."

—Coco Chanel

Dean Thompson

Marketing Director

{ *"Whatever it is that feels like it comes naturally to you, try to embrace that. For me, it was writing and a love of the way things look."* }

Job Description

Dean works as marketing director for a retail furniture company. "The ultimate goal of marketing for my company is to position our company in the consumer's mind as the furniture resource to turn to for design assistance, great selection, value, and service. My goal is to reach the customer through a variety of media to communicate that corporate message."

A Day on the Job

Checks e-mail. "So much of my correspondence is done via e-mail now." • Organizes her projects and works on those with immediate deadlines first. "My job is a lot like being an account executive for an advertising agency where I'm the person who is keeping the project going at all times." • Researches the market to find the best audience to target her efforts, "trying to identify people in the general population who have those same characteristics as our customers." • Writes copy for promotional items such as brochures, videos, press releases, promotional signage, hang tags, magazine advertisements, direct-mail campaigns, and e-mail blasts. "A typical day may be working to develop copy and a promotion for an e-mail blast or modifying copy on our Web site." • Produces and coordinates production of promotional items; this includes working with graphic designers, photographers, and printers. • On days that Dean is working away from her home office, she might be attending corporate meetings, coordinating seminars for customers, or overseeing a marketing program she initiated.

Job Likes

Dean is able to work from home in her current position. "I tend to really be able to focus on these types of activities… when it's a quiet environment. And at home, that really works for me because there aren't those constant interruptions." • "I love the diversity of the activity. Nothing is ever the same. The projects all differ." • "I love going from a conceptual idea through to having a finished product."

Job Challenges
"I'm really fortunate. I don't have a lot of dislikes." Her biggest frustration is that there are "not enough hours in the day." Time constraints keep her from doing everything she wants for a project.

Steps to Current Job
- University of North Carolina at Chapel Hill; Bachelor of Arts in Journalism.
- Sales job for one year.
- Meredith College in Raleigh, North Carolina; Bachelor of Science in Interior Design.
- Consumer Marketing Coordinator for a furniture company for two years.
- Furniture sales for two years.
- Decorative fabric sales for one year.
- Marketing consultant for a retirement-home developer for one year.
- Director of marketing for a furniture company for five years.
- Marketing director for a furniture retailer.

Advice
"Follow your natural loves. Whatever it is that feels like it comes naturally to you, try to embrace that. For me, it was writing and a love of the way things look. And while I didn't know what it was that I would ultimately want to do, I did know that I liked those two things." Dean feels that it is important to get a good formal education in what you like to do. She also adds, "one thing that's proven valuable to me is participating in internships, volunteering with organizations that are related to your field." Some of Dean's job offers have been through contacts she met while volunteering.

"Ease up on yourself. Be thoughtful, do your research, try your best to figure it out; but at those junctures, at some point, you just have to take a leap of faith and know that things are going to unfold in ways that you can't really foresee at that moment. Rarely are those decisions ones that are going to affect you until the day you retire."

Helpful Personality Traits
Enthusiastic, organized, excellent communication skills, including good writing skills and able to work well with others.

Hobbies & Interests
Outdoor activities, specifically hiking and canoeing, reading, and working on her house (decorating and gardening).

Deb Sweeney Whitmore

Outdoor Educator

{ *"You're basically at the whim of Mother Nature. She can either give you a beating with rain and lightning and cold temperatures, or she can really make it easy for you."* }

Outdoor educator Deb Whitmore shows off the gourmet calzones prepared by her class in the wilderness of the Wind River range, Wyoming.

Job Description
"I take students into the wilderness to learn about outdoor skills and how to work within a group of individuals." Deb teaches her students technical outdoor skills and environmental awareness while also working on personal growth and group development. The majority of her students are college age or between the ages of 20 and 30, but students can range anywhere from 14 years old and up. The outdoor sessions are anywhere from five days to 78 days long.

A Day on the Job
Designs the course for each session. • Teaches technical expedition skills, "which includes activities like rock climbing and white-water canoeing." • Teaches environmental skills, which includes "leave no trace" ethics and natural environment

information—"how we as a visitor in the wilderness can leave it the most untouched possible." • Manages the risks of each adventure by making sure all safety precautions are taken—"if we're rock climbing, making sure that everybody's got their harness on correctly. Making sure they've got their helmets on and their knots are tied." • Shares group-development strategies with students to develop personal and group growth—"giving them some tools as to how to work as a group within the outdoors." • Repairs and maintains gear and shelters. • Teaches outdoor-living skills such as food preparation for each meal, building shelters, and first aid. "A lot of people think that it's catered, but it's not."

Job Likes
Obviously, Deb enjoys being in the outdoors. • Not only does Deb get to teach the skills for outdoor activities, she also gets to participate in them. "It's a nice perk." • Deb enjoys meeting new people. • Days can be very long and "seeing the sun rise and set" in one day is rewarding.

Job Challenges
"You're basically at the whim of Mother Nature. She can either give you a beating with rain and lightning and cold temperatures, or she can really make it easy for you." • "The hours can be long. It's a 24/7 job." • "It can be difficult and stressful at times."

Steps to Current Job
- Crewe and Alsager College in Cheshire, United Kingdom; Bachelor of Science in Sports and Exercise Science. Worked at camps in New England during the summer.
- North Carolina Outward Bound Instructor and National Outdoor Leadership School (NOLS) Instructor. Each requires a training course.

Advice
"Have your own personal wilderness adventures" by joining sports clubs, getting outside, and doing the outdoor activities that interest you. By engaging in the activities you like, you'll gain experience and confidence, which helps you as a guide. "You need to be super comfortable when you're out there guiding students."

Looking back on her journals, Deb remembers an inspirational quote: "What you do today is important as you are exchanging a day of your life for it." She also feels that it is important to have a support group of women to hang out with and to share adventures. Deb's field is predominantly male, especially within the more technically challenging arenas such as ice climbing and mountaineering. She finds that when she spends time with a group of women, the experience is more of a self-growing experience where she can develop who she is and gain confidence.

Helpful Personality Traits
Energetic, confident, possess good communication skills, humble, and self-directed.

Hobbies & Interests
Mountain and road biking; bike maintenance (building and repairing); canoeing; kayaking; trying to live a healthy, simple life; and home renovation.

Debby Plexico

Medical/Surgical Floor Nurse

{ *"Nursing isn't just about healing wounds, it's about healing the soul and the spirit, too."* }

Job Description
Debby works in a hospital and takes care of patients recovering from surgery and patients needing general medical care.

A Day on the Job
Debby "picks up her patients." This means she either listens to an audio report or speaks with the night nurse, who updates her about their conditions. She is usually responsible for six patients. • Visits each patient and assesses their mental and physical condition. "I'll spend about 15 minutes in the room talking to the patient." • Gives medications. • Carries out doctor's orders; this might include preparing the patient for surgery, hanging new IV medications, changing their medication, or arranging for X rays. • Usually has 30 minutes for lunch—"which sometimes we don't get because the day is so busy." • Documents on the computer *everything* she does and everything that happens to her patients. "Nursing is extremely detailed work." • Tape records a report about her patients for the next nursing shift. Debby works a 12-hour shift.

Job Likes
"I like that every day is completely different." • "I like that every day there is something new to learn. There is always a new disease or a new way of treating a person… and that's what keeps the job fresh." • "I love my schedule. What I

feel is that if I have to work full-time, I would rather only show up to work three days a week and do 12, 13, or 14 hours in a day than go to work five days a week." • "I really like that it's not just nursing... much of the work that we do is almost like social work. We offer a great deal of moral support for those patients."

Job Challenges

"Probably the only bit I don't like is the doctors who aren't respectful." It can be challenging to work with a doctor who does not have a good bedside manner or does not respect the nurses.

Steps to Current Job
- University of London, Bachelor of Arts in Education.
- Elementary teacher at the British School in Tehran, Iran, for two years.
- Elementary teacher at the British School in Copenhagen, Denmark, for six months.
- Co-director for a realty company for 10 years.
- Stay-at-home mom.
- Preschool teacher for two years.
- Preschool director for two years.
- Executive director for an education foundation for four years.
- Development (fund-raising) for general administration at a university for two years, where she secured funds for the Center for International Understanding, a public service program of The University of North Carolina at Chapel Hill. During this time, Debby took pre-requisites for nursing school.
- Wake Technical Community College, Raleigh, North Carolina; Associate Degree in Nursing (ADN).
- Medical/surgical floor nurse.

Advice

Debby believes that you might be more satisfied and successful at nursing if before you start working, you get some world and life experience first. "It's a job that needs a significant amount of maturity. It's a very hard, physical job and also quite stressful... dealing with people in distress... you need to have some under-standing of the world. I think to go out in the world and do other things first and then go into nursing, you may enjoy the job better. That doesn't mean to say that you shouldn't train early and then say take that training and go do *Peace Corps* or do some kind of mission work. Nursing isn't just about healing wounds, it's about healing the soul and the spirit, too."

"Experiment. Don't think that you are just going to do one thing. Travel, do that semester abroad at the very least. The most important thing you can learn about yourself and your country is to take yourself out of your country because when you come back, you will see your country in a different light. And you will probably love it even more. But you really do need to see how the rest of the world lives so that you have a greater appreciation for your own country and what you have. Learn about the rest of the world." Debby suggests that while you are exploring the world, have that college degree so that you can be a participator, not just an observer. You can learn about other people and cultures, and at the same time give back to them, helping to make the world a better place.

Helpful Personality Traits
Patient, detail-oriented, mature, desire to serve, giving, nonjudgmental, not a whiner, and not faint of heart.

Hobbies & Interests
Reading, travel, current affairs, spending time with family, being outdoors at the beach, and a love of nature.

> *Peace Corps* is, according to its Web site, "an agency of the federal government devoted to world peace and friendship." Peace Corps volunteers are sent to countries around the world to work on "issues ranging from AIDS education, information technology, and environmental preservation." (For more information, see www.peacecorps.gov.)

Debra Sasser

North Carolina District Court Judge

{ *"If I am in traffic court, I may have 1,000 to 1,200 cases a day."* }

Job Description
Debra is "the decision-maker in many different kinds of disputes—everything from criminal to family." She goes on to explain, "A district court judge is the

District court judge Debra Sasser takes a quick call before heading back to the bench.

jury and the judge in a lot of different types of matters." In North Carolina, where Debra works, district court is divided into four categories: civil, criminal, *magistrate,* and juvenile. Debra hears civil cases such as divorce, custody, and child support, and cases involving disputes over less than $10,000. She also hears criminal cases involving misdemeanors and infractions, as well as juvenile cases that involve children under the age of 16 who are delinquent and children under the age of 18 who are undisciplined, dependent, neglected, or abused.

A Day on the Job
Listens to people "talking about facts and circumstances of a dispute." Oftentimes Debra also hears attorneys make legal arguments. The number of cases that she hears can vary, depending on which court Debra is serving on a particular day. She says, "If I am in traffic court *(disposition courtroom)*... I may have 1,000 to 1,200 cases a day. In a regular, traffic criminal courtroom, I might have 300 to 400... but, I did two matters (cases) today. So, it really depends on which courtroom I'm in." • Makes a decision "as to the resolution or outcome" of a matter.

Job Likes
"It's an opportunity for me to do something to give back to the community." • Debra loves that she is fulfilling a long-term goal of hers—to be the person, "who makes the decisions—right or wrong."

Job Challenges

"The sheer number of cases… we don't short-change any matter, but when you run out of time, people who have been sitting there all morning get a new court date and have to come back."

Steps to Current Job

- Oklahoma State University in Stillwater; Bachelor of Science in Sociology with an emphasis in Criminology.
- Computer systems analyst for nine years.
- University of North Carolina at Chapel Hill Law School, Juris Doctorate.
- Associate attorney for law firms for six years.
- Legal counsel for the state *Guardian ad Litem* office for two years (see page 65 for a definition).
- Owner of mediation and arbitration practice for three years.
- District court judge.

Advice

"Figure out what kind of judge you want to be, and try to get as much work as an advocate attorney in that area as you can… but it's not a job that you earn on your merit, in all honesty. It's an elected position." So Debra says that it's important to determine what you need to do to get elected. Find out whose support and endorsements you're going to need. "Network with your peers. Become someone whose name is familiar. You have to be willing to realize that it's going to take more to get the job than your abilities."

"I think that you can go one of two routes. You can either set your mind on something, and just plow ahead… or you can be a little bit more open. I think my advice would be to come up with a goal, but don't limit yourself to your path on how to get there. There may be other opportunities on the way… that turn out to be something that's going to help you when you get to your goal."

Helpful Personality Traits

Debra says that any personality will work on the bench, but you need to be approachable, decisive, self-tolerant, and able to show restraint, and you must want to do the right thing.

Hobbies & Interests

Family time, reading mystery and crime novels, and working out.

Magistrates, in North Carolina, are appointed officers of district court. They accept guilty pleas for minor misdemeanors and traffic violations, and accept waivers of trial for worthless-check cases, among other things. In civil cases, the magistrate is authorized to try small claims involving up to $4,000, including landlord-eviction cases. (For more information, see www.nccourts.org/Courts/Trial/District/Default.asp.)

A *disposition courtroom* is one where most traffic and misdemeanor criminal defendants appear for their initial scheduled court dates. It is an "all-day" court-room open from 7:45 a.m. to 3:30 p.m. (with no break for the judge). Only guilty pleas or deferred prosecutions are handled by the judge in that courtroom, so things move quickly.

Diane Jacober

Product Support Engineer (Mechanical Engineer)

{ *"I like to solve problems. I've always enjoyed puzzles and mysteries."* }

Job Description

As a product support engineer for a large chemical corporation, Diane uses her *mechanical engineering* knowledge to improve or design a mechanical process that either enhances an existing product or develops a new one. "It's like an investigation. You have a product, there's a problem with it. You look at what the deficiencies are and use that as clues to go back into the process. So I would either make adjustments in the mechanics or the chemist would make adjustments in the chemical process." Her last project was to improve the mammography film made by her company.

A Day on the Job

Gathers information from customers about problems they are having with an existing product. In the mammography film project, "I would go to the customer, see how they use it, understand their needs. What's important about the film? What's important about the end product? What do we need for the next generation?" • Relays customer feedback and her own test results to company scientists—"give input to the scientists who are developing the product." • Runs tests on the improved products. • Presents customers with product adjustments for their feedback. • Makes more adjustments according to customer suggestions. • Writes all product information for the customer, marketing brochures, and Web site. • Fields questions from customers about existing products.

Job Likes
"I like to solve problems. I've always enjoyed puzzles and mysteries." • "I like variety, and monotony drives me crazy." Diane enjoys the "variety of challenges to take a design concept and bring it to reality."

Job Challenges
Diane says when testing a product, she sometimes gets "in a pattern of doing the same thing every day," and she doesn't like that. • "The first thing I did in the morning was listen to all the phone calls I got overnight about problems people are having. It was a bad way to start the day," Diane laughs.

Steps to Current Job
- Dartmouth College in Hanover, New Hampshire; Bachelor of Arts in Engineering.
- Thayer School of Engineering on the Dartmouth College campus; Bachelor of Science in Mechanical Engineering and Master's in Mechanical Engineering.
- Worked for a chemical corporation company, where she worked in the following positions:
  - Process engineer for two years.
  - Manufacturing engineer for a year and a half.
  - Project engineer in south India for one year.
  - Project engineer in medical imaging for three years.
  - Product support engineer for six years.*

Advice
"If you are somebody who likes math and science, I think it's a great opportunity for women because there aren't very many women in engineering and science. Women have a lot to add in the manufacturing world. They have a different viewpoint, good ideas. We need more women in that kind of environment."

"Do something you like to do because if you are happy, you are successful." Don't succumb to pressure of what someone else might think is right for you; it has to be what you like to do.

---

*Due to facility relocation, Diane has decided to take time off and work as a full-time mom. If Diane does not return to mechanical engineering, she is contemplating working as a French teacher.

Helpful Personality Traits

Curious, persistent, and an aptitude for and enjoyment of science and math.

Hobbies & Interests

Hiking with family, running with friends, reading with her children, and conducting science experiments with her children.

> Diane defines *mechanical engineering* as problem-solving; using a combination of math and science for "designing mechanical processes for production" in an affordable and efficient manner.

CONFIDENCE AND PEOPLE SKILLS

Confidence and being a people person are beneficial personality traits recommended by many Firestarters. If you are interested in one of these jobs, but you don't feel like you possess confidence or good people skills, don't fret. Both of these characteristics can be learned or improved.

The more education and experience you have, the more confidence you build and the better you will be able to relate to others. There can be many different levels of being a "people person." Maybe you are not a Ms. Bubbly, cheerleader type by nature; that's okay. You can develop the skills needed to communicate professionally through experience and by taking communication courses.

Donna Helms

PGA (Professional Golfers' Association) Teaching Professional

{ *"You're not going to play a song after four piano lessons. The same with golf. You're not going to shoot par after four lessons, but you will have the concept of what a good swing looks and feels like."* }

Golf professional Donna Helms teaches her student the fundamentals of the sport.

Job Description

Donna describes her job this way: "There are professional golfers and golf pro-fessionals. Professional golfers are the ones who play, and golf professionals are the ones who teach others to play." She teaches people of all different ages and skill levels and says, "I have two students who are three years old, and my oldest student was a lady who was 83 when she won the Super Senior National Championship." Donna wants to make the distinction that she is not certified by the LPGA (Ladies Professional Golf Association). She is one of only 1,000 or so women golf professionals who are members of the PGA (Donna says she chose the PGA rather than the LPGA because she was impressed with its continuing-education program). When one realizes that the PGA is the largest sports organization in the world, with more than 26,000 members, Donna's accomplishment is pretty remarkable.

A Day on the Job

Performs three clinics a week to market her services—"I do ladies' clinics, men's clinics, and junior clinics." • Sells four-lesson packages to clients/students, but often people will continue taking lessons after the fourth one ends. "I compare it to taking piano lessons. You're not going to play a song after four piano les-sons. The same with golf. You're not going to shoot par after four lessons, but you will have the concept of what a good swing looks and feels like." • Assesses her student at the first lesson. "It's sort of a test every time I have a new student because you have to see what their limitations and strengths are." • Videotapes her student to look for problems in form, and so on. "I break their swing down and show them where they are. By comparing their swing to the top players, they catch on to the fundamentals much quicker." • Teaches golf fundamentals. "I show them if they can maintain certain angles in their arms and shoulders and their wrists, then they can play." • "I usually start around 10:00 a.m., and the range closes at 7:00 p.m., and it's kind of nonstop in season; I book a lesson every 30 minutes." Golf season goes from May until early October, and in the off-season, Donna works as a nutritional consultant.

Job Likes
Donna says she enjoys "the satisfaction of knowing that I'm molding golf swings and creating really satisfied students." • Donna likes the relationships that she builds with her students. "You get personally involved with these people. They like to talk to you. They like to tell you things." • "I like being around people with diverse lifestyles. There are so many neat people out there."

Job Challenges
The long hours in season keep Donna from spending time with her daughter. • "It is seasonal. You have to scramble around and figure out how to make a living the other four or five months." • "I can't have any down time. I have to be just as happy and glad to see my 6 o'clock [p.m. appointment] as I was to see my 10 o'clock. You've got to give them all you've got because they're paying you."

Steps to Current Job
- Donna attended a business school in Charlotte, North Carolina, for two years and said, "I tried to get into business, but my heart just wasn't into it. I'm an outside person. I'm just a sports person. I believe in being active."
- Appalachian State University, Boone, North Carolina; two years toward a business degree. Donna took up golf when she was 26 and really enjoyed it. At age 30, she earned a full golf scholarship. She said, "I was the oldest woman. I was a late bloomer."
- Teaching professional for various golf courses since leaving Appalachian 24 years ago. In the off-season, Donna consults people, especially cancer patients, on alternative treatments for physical/medical ailments. "I don't treat, and I don't diagnose; and that's my disclaimer. But, I do give people things to read… especially cancer patients, and we've had some success with them doing alternative things."

Advice
Donna thinks that it's important to decide whether you want to teach or play. If you want to play, she says to start early. "Even then [in college] I knew that I couldn't be competitive with those younger girls. They hit the ball too far. I was a good amateur player, but I've never played professionally. You have to know

that it's what you want to do. You need to understand what golf is, what teaching is." In order to be a member of the PGA, you have to take a Player Ability Test (PAT) and attend required classes. For the PAT, women have to play from the same tees as men. "Now, playing from the back tees like the men, women were given five more shots per round, but you had to shoot a target score."

Donna says, "Just stay focused and have some kind of goal. Write it down. Even if you're 16 or 60, you're going to forget. You're going to be diverted by life. Everybody is blindsided once in a while, but just get up and stay the course; know what you want and go after it."

Helpful Personality Traits
Good listener, compassionate, empathetic ("When your student hurts, you hurt"), nurturing, firm but gentle, technical (but don't go overboard), and a "love of people and life."

Hobbies & Interests
Spending time with her daughter and family, reading and relaxing in the sauna.

Doris Sargent

Nutrition Consultant and Registered Dietician (R.D.)

"Nutrition is such a changing area. So what came out two or three years ago is definitely changing."

Job Description
Doris works in the Nutrition Services Branch of North Carolina's Department of Public Health. Here she trains elementary school teachers about proper nutrition for students. The goal is to have the teachers take this knowledge back to their classrooms and teach their students what they've learned. Doris also works with the child nutrition staffs (food preparers) of all schools, kindergarten through 12, to teach them how to plan and prepare nutritious meals.

Doris' job is just one of a number that you can get if you have a degree in nutrition with R.D. status. Hospitals, sports teams, and nursing homes often have a registered dietician on-site who assesses nutritional needs and plans nutritional programs. There are even opportunities to act as an independent consultant helping people on an individual basis to determine a nutritional "plan of attack."

A Day on the Job

Answers nutrition questions from school-system employees, teachers, and parents, either by phone or e-mail. • Prepares training presentations—creates PowerPoint presentations and handouts. Over the course of a year, Doris gives an average of one presentation a month. • Attends meetings or participates in conference calls. The school system that Doris works for is a big organization, and she interacts with different groups within it. For example, "The physical activity branch, they also have an interest in nutrition, so we organize things together." • Acts as a technical assistant for schools. "We have a program called 'Winner's Circle' where items that are served in school cafeterias are labeled this way if they meet a certain nutritional criteria. So, we have a lot of people calling in checking to see if the products meet it." Doris helps them analyze the particular item of food, and she helps them determine the best way to promote the food's "Winner's Circle" status. • Updates her knowledge of nutrition continually. "Nutrition is such a changing area. So what came out two or three years ago is definitely changing."

Job Likes

"I enjoy the subject area because I think it's challenging." • "I enjoy the people that I work with." • "It's always different. It's not mundane, and I like that. If somebody likes routine—to come in everyday and do the same thing—it's not for them."

Job Challenges

Doris works for state government and says, "There's always politics… for example, with the food guide pyramid that just came out, there's such heavy influence from the commodity groups." • "Another thing in government—things move so slowly."

Steps to Current Job

- Mansfield University, Mansfield, Pennsylvania; Bachelor of Science in Home Economics.
- Home economics teacher for two years.
- Stay-at-home mom for five years.
- Owner/operator of a dairy farm and milk-processing plant that had a restaurant on the premises. "It was seven days a week, 365 days a year. So, when my kids were in college, I said, 'This is it.' And, I went back to school and got the nutrition degree."
- Mansfield University, Bachelor of Science in Nutrition and a Master's in Nutrition. Doris earned her Registered Dietician certification as an undergraduate.
- *Registered dietician* for six months.

- Nutrition educator for five years.
- Nutrition program manager for seven years.
- Nutrition consultant with the Nutrition Services Branch in the Department of Public Health and working toward her Ph.D. at North Carolina State University in Raleigh in Adult and Agriculture Extension Education.

Advice

Doris would recommend that you get your master's in nutrition if this is a job that appeals to you. "A lot of schools offer that complete program. You can do the master's the same time as your undergraduate."

"People have many different careers in their life. If we're not happy in something, we can move on to something else." For this reason, Doris says, "Don't burn any bridges… because you never know when you're going to come back and need that person." She also encourages you to "take a risk. If it feels right, go for it. Think, 'What would be the worst thing if I failed?' If the worst thing is not really that bad, go for it."

When asked whether she would change anything about her life or career path, Doris didn't miss a beat answering, "I would have spent more time with my children when they were little. Those kids are only young for so long… but you have plenty of time in your life to have that career, and we're spanning our careers longer now."

Helpful Personality Traits

Get along with people, empathetic, aggressive, outspoken, ambitious, and extroverted.

Hobbies & Interests

Tennis, bicycling, staying physically active, cooking, doing hand crafts, and family time.

> A *registered dietician* must attend a college or university that offers a bachelor's degree in nutrition. After completing specific coursework, identified by the American Dietetic Association, she is eligible to sit for an exam. Once this exam is passed, she is given her Registered Dietician certification.

Elaine Marshall

North Carolina Secretary of State

{ *"My boss is the 8.5 million people of North Carolina."* }

North Carolina Secretary of State Elaine Marshall gives a commencement address to her alma mater, Campbell University.

Photo courtesy of Campbell University photographer Bennett Scarborough.

Job Description

Elaine is an elected official who oversees the North Carolina Department of State. She quips, "This agency's business is business." Her agency's mission statement best explains its function: "To serve and protect citizens, the business community and governmental agencies by facilitating business activities, by providing accurate and timely information, and by preserving documents and records." When asked who she reports to, Elaine's response is, "My boss is the 8.5 million people of North Carolina." Her term is four years, and there is no limit to the number of times she can be reelected.

A Day on the Job

Goes through her mail. • Meets with her staff to discuss issues that have been brought to their attention. Elaine prioritizes which issues her office will handle. • Ensures that her office serves as an "honest broker" and record-keeper for business transactions. For example, if a business wants to apply for a trademark in North Carolina or wants to incorporate, it does this through the Secretary of State's office, and the office keeps those records on file. • Sets policies. Elaine refers to an instance where she determined that the punishment for a certain security scam was not severe enough and did not deter people from committing that crime. So, she spearheaded a request to the General Assembly (the North Carolina legislature) to change the law, making the punishment for that crime more severe. • "I'm the one who listens to the bankers when they say 'You know we would be more economically competitive if....' And a lot of times that 'if' falls in my lap." • Acts as a spokesperson. "I'm the chief cheerleader, public relations person for this agency." Among the many groups that she speaks to are lawyers, bankers, CPAs, civic clubs, hospital associations, and General Assembly committees. She also speaks to members of youth groups to motivate and inspire them to think about their future. • In some circumstances, Elaine may "sit as a judge."

Job Likes

"I like problem-solving." Prior to becoming the Secretary of State, Elaine enjoyed the problem-solving that came with being a lawyer in a private practice. Her current position allows her the same kind of problem-solving on a "much larger scope and level." She works to find solutions to challenges like, "How do I make life easier for businesses operating in North Carolina? How do I make the experience between the citizen and government easy?" • "I do like the fact of being the first woman and having that little footnote of history." Elaine is not only the first woman Secretary of State for North Carolina, but she is also the first woman to be elected to any North Carolina statewide executive office. • "I truly believe that other women will have better chances in this state because I broke a glass ceiling, and others can come through it now."

Job Challenges

Even though Elaine's office takes in a large amount of money for the state, she has to "beg for the money back to run my office." • "I dislike the disfunctionality of the legislative process." The "hurry up and wait" approach is frustrating.

Steps to Current Job

- University of Maryland in College Park; Bachelor of Science in Textiles and Clothing.

- Home economics teacher in the public school system for one year.
- Home economics instructor for a community college for seven years.
- Co-owner of a book and gift store while working as a teacher/instructor.
- Owner and decorator for a fabric and decorating store for four years.
- Campbell University School of Law in Buies Creek, North Carolina; Juris Doctorate.
- Lawyer in a private practice for 16 years. She was also a part-time lawyer during her time as State Senator and during her campaigns.
- North Carolina State Senator for one term.
- North Carolina Secretary of State, currently in her third term.

Advice

If holding a public office is your goal, Elaine advises you to "sit and watch the political process up front" to find out whether you have a "taste" for that kind of environment. "You've got to have a thick skin. You've got to have patience. You've got to not take things personally." She suggests becoming a page for the state senate, house, or governor and to participate in student government and clubs such as 4-H, church groups, or in some form of government/democratic environment. Elaine also stresses the importance of getting a solid education and developing good writing and oral communication skills because they are important in any career.

Drawing from her law school experience, Elaine says "stretch yourself. Successfully completing something that's easy is a shallow reward, but successfully completing something that is really a stretch goal for you, that's about as exhilarating as it gets." When Elaine decided to go to law school, it was the first time in her life that she was not totally confident in what she was doing. She was not accepted right away into law school, and when she started, she struggled. Not until the middle of her second year did she get the hang of it and start winning awards. Elaine also advises, "Believe in yourself and listen to your gut. If something feels queasy and fishy, it probably is. Even if everybody else is doing it, let it alone."

Helpful Personality Traits

Perseverance, an understanding of human nature, ability to think on your feet, empathetic, compassionate, and a willingness to listen.

Hobbies & Interests

Cooking, sewing, gardening, sailing, and watching sports.

To learn more about Elaine's job, visit www.sosnc.com.

Erin Pawlus

District Manager—Retail Fashion Industry

{ *"Mainly my job consists of strategic thinking—thinking ahead of time and planning accordingly."* }

Job Description
Erin is responsible for driving up sales volume and developing management teams for her company. Several stores report to her, and she in turn, reports to a regional manager and to a vice president.

A Day on the Job
Participates in conference calls at the beginning of each week to touch base with all of her stores (reviews previous weeks' results, sets goals for the upcoming week, and reviews management development plans). • Eighty percent of Erin's time is spent in the stores that report to her. She feels that she can get a better idea of the "temperature" of a store if she's witnessing it from the customer's and sales associate's points of view. • Ensures that all policies and procedures are adhered to, that the customer experience is consistent store to store, and that managers are setting development goals for themselves and for their teams.

Job Likes
For Erin, the customer interaction is the best part of her job. "Selling and not just to make the sale, but to sell something to customers that they truly love," is something that gives her a lot of satisfaction. • Erin enjoys what she calls "people development." She likes helping her employees set and achieve professional goals.

Job Challenges
Erin says, "People are unique… and what makes managing people fun is that everyone is managed differently. Sometimes it's frustrating when you are trying to ensure consistency. I work well with people who strive for the best results and have an incredible work ethic. When this is not there, my job becomes harder."

Steps to Current Job
• Indiana University in Gary, Bachelor of Science in Business Management.

- Erin has worked for the same company since 1992 in the following positions:
  - Part-time sales associate for three months.
  - Full-time sales associate for three months.
  - Part-time assistant manager for six months.
  - Full-time assistant manager for one year.
  - Associate manager, low-volume store, for 18 months.
  - Store manager, low-volume store, for two years.
  - Store Manager, high-volume store, for two years.
  - Store manager, flagship building (top 10 in company), for two years.
  - Area Manager for two years.
  - District manager.

Advice

"Have patience. Often in retail careers you are rushed along because of immediate openings. Take time to learn the skills along the way. Find a company that has proven longevity and that is respected in the industry, not only for its customer service, but also for how well they train and develop their managers and sales associates."

Erin says that if you have a job now, "even if it's not in your ideal career, learn everything you can from it. What works for you, what you would change? " She also says, "Try to learn something new every day. This will help you think differently when you start your career. Question everything—not to change everything, but to learn from your questions. Never settle on 'What was good enough yesterday is good enough for today.'"

Helpful Personality Traits

Charismatic, sense of urgency, goal oriented, strong work ethic, organized, and interested in fashion.

Hobbies & Interests

Reading, travel, and exploring her new city—Erin recently moved to New York.

Erinn Qualter Kelly

Equity Research, Managing Director

{ *"What better place for a woman to truly push herself to new levels than to be on Wall Street!"* }

Job Description
Erinn works for an investment bank in New York City where she is one of four managers who oversee a global staff of 375 employees made up of research analysts and associates who work for the analysts. Her staff researches publicly traded companies to find financial investment opportunities for their clients. Their client base is comprised of mutual fund companies, hedge funds, and individual investors. The sales force shares the research with clients, and the research is also used to make investments for Erinn's company.

A Day on the Job
Meets with analysts and reviews research ratings. • Produces productivity and budget analysis reports for her director. • Recruits staff for the department. • Gives sales presentations to clients and internal departments. • Travels internationally to research branch offices. • Works with senior members of the firm in strategic planning to increase the firm's profitability.

Job Likes
Erinn enjoys the high energy level and quick pace of her job. • Exposure to a wide variety of people inside the firm, her clients, and prospective clients is stimulating to Erinn. • She likes that her position allows her freedom to implement ideas quickly. • The financial compensation is an added incentive.

Job Challenges
Before joining the equity research management team, Erinn was a *bond trader* for the same company. To Erinn, managing is not as glamorous as being a bond trader. "A trading desk is the most exciting place on Wall Street to work; the wit is quick, the pressure is high, and the money flows. Needless to say, the perception of a trader is far 'cooler' than that of a manager." • "It is often difficult to take direction from a manager who is not in the trenches with you."

Steps to Current Job
- Fairfield University in Fairfield, Connecticut; Bachelor of Arts with a double major in Economics and Spanish.
- Trading desk assistant for a large investment bank for three years.
- Bond trader for the same company for five years.
- Manager of equity research for the same company for three years. During this time, Erinn took level one of the CFA (Chartered Financial Analyst) program, and she also took the Series 16 exam. These steps helped qualify her to work in equity research.
- Currently taking a leave of absence to stay home with her young children.

Advice
"Business degrees such as finance, economics, and statistics seem to be preferred over marketing and management degrees on Wall Street." Erinn says that a

degree from a large university known for its business school, specifically north-eastern schools, makes it easier to get your foot in the door on Wall Street. Firms recruit on these campuses more often than they do on smaller, lesser-known campuses. "Inquire about internships. Nothing beats experience." In college, meet all the recruiters who come to your campus and ask to spend a day at their firm. Talk with as many people at the firm as possible when you are there. Large Wall Street firms offer three main types of front-office training programs: investment banking, research, and sales and trading. Erinn's other Wall Street advice: "Once at the firm, never say no or show the slightest displeasure to the coffee runs, working in the back office, pricing trading books, or anything that could be perceived as below you. Be patient, yet assertive, and you'll get your day in the sun with lots of supporters behind you. Try not to hop around the street. The best traction for your career comes from building a strong network at one firm."

"My dad, from the time I was very little, taught me to ignore gender stereo-typing. 'Break the barrier' he used to say. What better place for a woman to truly push herself to new levels than to be on Wall Street! Bond trading is still a highly competitive, male-dominated, lucrative industry." When Erinn was a bond trader, there were 150 traders in her company; only three were women.

Helpful Personality Traits
Highly competitive, mathematically inclined, outgoing and personable, social, focused, hardworking, willing to make sacrifices, dedicated and motivated by financial compensation.

Hobbies & Interests
The global stock markets, business in general, mystery thrillers, raising her children to be good people with open minds, travel, and sports.

Bond traders locate and sell bonds to their clients and also make investments for their employer. Bonds are certificates sold by the government and corporations to raise money for projects. On a specific date, the bond is redeemable with a set amount of interest. Bonds are sometimes purchased for tax exemption purposes.

"Remember, Ginger Rogers did everything Fred Astaire did, but she did it backwards and in high heels."

—Faith Whittlesey

Gena Farris

Speech Therapist (Speech and Language Pathologist)

{ *"We teach them how to optimize the deficit that they have. You want to get them as independent and as functional as you can."* }

Job Description

Gena provides therapy to people with speech, language, cognitive, and swallowing problems. She works in the acute-care center of a hospital, where the majority of her patients are recovering from neurological disorders resulting from stroke or head injury or recovering from laryngeal cancer. "We are working to optimize their overall communication and swallowing functions."

A Day on the Job

Reviews information on new patients. These are usually high-priority cases because "nine times out of ten, what people are consulting us for are swallowing problems. That's a life-and-death situation." • Reviews her established caseload and prioritizes the order in which she'll visit each patient. • Provides patient care by evaluating their status, providing therapy and establishing a diet conducive to their problem. "When you do an evaluation, you're trying to figure out what their deficits are, but at the same time you are trying to figure out what their strengths are because a lot of times you have to use those to help compensate for what they're having problems with. We teach them how to optimize the deficit that they have. You want to get them as independent and as functional as you can." • Makes weekly rounds with the entire team of medical personnel involved in patient care. "It keeps everybody on the same page on what everybody is doing." • Supervises visiting students who shadow her for course credit.

Job Likes

Gena is a "people person" and enjoys the interaction she has with her patients, their families, and the hospital staff. • "Everybody is an individual, so you treat everybody differently," and Gena thinks this keeps her job interesting. • "I'm not stuck behind a desk all day." • Her schedule is somewhat flexible because her hours are not rigid.

Job Challenges

Because Gena works in a hospital, she has to work weekends and holidays. Even though she rotates this duty with other staff members, Gena says that working weekends can be difficult "if you have a spouse that works Monday through Friday... or if you have kids." • Gena says that although things are starting to change, presently her position is not paid as highly as comparable jobs such as occupational therapy or physical therapy.

Steps to Current Job

- North Carolina State University in Raleigh, Bachelor of Arts in Communications with a concentration in disorders.
- University of South Carolina in Columbia, Master of Speech Pathology (MSP).
- Clinical Fellowship Year (CFY), for approximately one year—this is required.
- Staff therapist for a rehab management facility.
- Staff therapist in rehab and brain injury at a hospital for two years.
- Clinical lead for acute speech pathology for a hospital. Gena worked her way up from staff therapist to clinical specialist to clinical lead.

Advice

It is helpful to know that the master's program is competitive, a GRE score is required, and you will need letters of recommendation. Gena points out that an undergraduate degree in Speech Pathology is not required for acceptance into a Speech Pathology master's program. She thinks that having an undergraduate degree in something else broadens your horizons.

"Weed out what you definitely couldn't see yourself doing," and then start looking at careers that might interest you. Gena took many introductory classes while at North Carolina State. One of them was an introduction to communication disorders. She was intrigued by this class, and it lead her to her career.

Helpful Personality Traits

Should enjoy school, compassionate, empathetic, sympathetic, a people person, and enjoys life sciences.

Hobbies & Interests

Travel, spending time at the beach, water and snow skiing, television, and movies.

Ginger Poole

Actor

{ *"Sometimes as an actor we grasp for something to connect with a character, and for me a lot of times it's the shoes."* }

Ginger Poole's headshot, which she uses for auditions and playbills.
Credit: Courtesy Melissa Hamburg

Job Description

"Until an actor steps in, a script or a story or a monologue is simply ink on a page, and it takes the actor to put that to life and… make those words jump off the page." Ginger describes her job as a performer and a storyteller, someone who "brings life to words." She acts in *professional houses* throughout the Southeast. "When I'm not working on stage or on a production, my bread-and-butter money is teaching acting or dance."

A Day on the Job

Studies her character. If she's lucky, Ginger gets the script early and does her "homework" before rehearsals begin. "You use your dictionary for words that you're not familiar with or use your pronunciation guide if there's any word that you don't know how to say." • Starts rehearsals and begins memorizing lines. • Blocks the play with the director and the other actors—"where he wants you to walk or stand or sit." • Builds her character. "You still have to layer on the life of this person that you're creating, whether they're funny, or they're clumsy, or they may have a nervous tic. Sometimes as actors we grasp for something to connect with that character, and for me a lot of times it's the shoes." • Meshes all aspects of the production together. This includes all of the preceding, along with costumes, set design, props, and lighting. • Runs the production over and over until it clicks. • Performs the play. Most of Ginger's shows run between four and six weeks. • Teaches dance and acting when not performing. Ginger teaches in her community, and she also teaches master classes in some of the communities where she is performing. "This works hand in hand with being an actor. If you're teaching something, I think you're still honing your skills." • Markets and networks to find auditions and to meet contacts. "You have to think about marketing yourself as a product." She finds auditions through the actor's union and by networking within the theatre community. • Auditions for shows.

Job Likes

"I love people. I love meeting new people." Ginger is "plopped" into a new community with each show and this allows her to meet new actors, directors, and communities. • "Not to sound corny… but I love meeting the people on the page." Ginger especially likes working on roles when she is not familiar with a character and does not have a preconceived idea of how that character should act. • "I love working with others as far as the collaboration as an art. Just one person couldn't do it. You truly have to work as a team. It's not a me, me, me profession."

Job Challenges

"The huge challenge is to realize there's nothing consistent about this profession. When the show's over, you're unemployed." • "You have to stay energized and excited about putting yourself out there again."

Steps to Current Job
- The University of West Georgia in Carrollton; Bachelor of Arts in Theatre, minor in Sociology.
- Assistant artistic director at a theatre for one year.
- The University of Southern Mississippi in Hattiesburg; Master of Fine Arts in Performance. Interned at a professional theatre during the summer, where she earned points for her *equity card*.
- Actor for professional theatres, dance and acting teacher.

Advice

"In this business you have to be open and okay with rejection and sometimes a lot of it. Every audition and every interview is another chance to perform." Ginger advises, "Always be as open as you possibly can. No matter how much schooling, no matter how many accolades or awards or recognition that you may get for your talent. Don't shut yourself off to new knowledge and new experiences." She also feels that it is important to "continue to go to classes, continue to go to shows, continue to read. There is a plethora of books and text and script for an actor. You broaden your knowledge of what's out there, you broaden your vocabulary and your mind."

"Have the confidence and the self-esteem to know that very few things in life are completely impossible. Set those goals, and even if they are just out of the ballpark... set 'em up there anyway. You'll be surprised at what you can achieve."

Helpful Personality Traits

Driven, creative, thick-skinned, a "giver," a people person, and "you have to have a little bit of gypsy in you maybe; sometimes you'll live out of your suitcase."

Hobbies & Interests

Theatre—"Not just doing it, but I love to go to theatre. Any type of theatre"; traveling; reading; and "I love children."

Professional houses are theatres that use equity actors in their productions and follow the guidelines set by the Actor's Equity Association (AEA).

Equity actors are members of the labor union, Actors' Equity Association (AEA). Actors must earn a certain number of points to be admitted into the AEA and then receive their *equity card*. Points are earned for each week interning or working as a non-equity performer. For more information, go to www.actorsequity.org.

Gwen Beatty

Geologist

{ *"It's almost like a puzzle. My job is like being an adult and being paid to play."* }

Job Description

"I'm a geologist, and I work identifying groundwater contamination." Gwen works with state-contracted consultants to locate possible water-contamination

sites around her state. Because the results that she finds can either affect someone's personal water supply or can possibly affect an entire town or city's water
supply, Gwen takes her job very seriously.

A Day on the Job

In the Office

Assigns tasks to consultants. • Plans contamination assessments and determines
next steps for contaminated sites. • Interprets results from field work. • Oversees
consultants. Gwen has three contracts that are her responsibility, and she is currently working on 40 sites.

In the Field

Walks sites with consultants looking for potential sources of contamination. • Determines where to test soil and groundwater based on the history of
a site. "Sometimes there may have been 100 different businesses (past and present) that have been in an area." Knowing the history helps Gwen and her team
determine where and what type of contamination is likely. • Discusses where
the subcontractors that her consultants have hired will drill for water and install
temporary monitoring wells. • Checks monitoring wells for any contamination. • Sends soil and water samples to accredited lab.

Job Likes

"I love my job. I absolutely love my job." Gwen says, "I like the fact that I went
to college for six years [four years undergraduate; two years master's]… and I
actually learned something that I can take out into the field and use." • "I like
the fact that I have some days in the office. I like the fact that some days I'm outdoors. I may be out in the field walking through beautiful wooded areas." • "It's
the type of job where you don't know everything there is to know. You're always
learning. It's almost like a puzzle. My job is like being an adult and being paid
to play." • "The other thing that I like about my job is I have an excellent rap-
port with the guys I work with."

Job Challenges

"I don't really dislike anything about it," Gwen says, but she also says, "I would
prefer if there were more women in geology. We women are a civilizing influence
on men. They behave better when there are more of us." • "What I do is always
in the public eye, and I must admit, sometimes when politicians get involved
they can be a pain. They mean well, but they don't necessarily understand what
I do."

Steps to Current Job
- University of North Carolina at Chapel Hill; Dental Assistant program.
- Dental assistant for three years. "I hated it. It was boring [to Gwen]."
- Gwen married at an early age and held odd jobs for four years, helping put her now ex-husband through school.
- St. Petersburg (Florida) Junior College for two years before transferring to a four-year school.
- University of South Florida at Tampa; Bachelor of Science in Geology.
- University of Florida at Gainesville; Master of Science in Geology.
- Worked in the petroleum industry for 12 years.
- Environmental Specialist III for the State of Florida.

Advice
"I would suggest if you want to become a geologist that you take as much math, chemistry, and physics that you can possibly take."

Helpful Personality Traits
Analytical, good problem solver, self-confident, and a good sense of humor.

Hobbies & Interests
Canoeing, kayaking, backpacking, hiking, current events, and cooking.

Holly K. Dressman

Assistant Research Professor and Director of the Duke DNA Microarray Core Facility

"I am interested in applying gene-expression profiles to help better understand the development and progression of cancer."

Job Description
Holly is the director of the Duke Microarray Core Facility. This facility develops major research projects that use the analysis of *DNA microarrays* to study *gene expression*. Her research focus is studying gene expressions to investigate breast, ovarian, and lung cancer development, progression, and response to therapy. These studies are used to develop clinical applications. Her position at Duke is in the Department of Molecular Genetics and Microbiology and in the Institute of Genome Sciences and Policy.

A Day on the Job

Consults with Duke investigators about experimental design and analysis of microarrays. Investigators include professors, clinicians, post-doctoral fellows, clinical fellows, residents, medical students, and graduate students. • Lectures about the technology and applications of microarrays to Duke investigators. Holly speaks at local universities and at nationwide meetings. She also lectures undergraduate and graduate courses at local universities. • Directs the microarray lab activities—which includes overseeing lab personnel, productivity, development of microarrays, microarray assays, and database management—and provides analysis support in understanding the progression of cancer and various other diseases. • Writes papers and grants to help fund research that involves gene-expression studies.

Job Likes

Holly loves that her job combines her interests of science and technology. • She enjoys "the challenges of pursuing clinical trials that involve gene-expression profiling." • "The work environment—which includes scientists, computational biologists, statisticians and clinicians—provides an exciting, stimulating, and enjoyable atmosphere." • Holly enjoys "the collaboration with other scientists and clinicians that are based on translational *genomics*." In other words, she likes working as a team to find treatments based on their discoveries.

Job Challenges

"The time commitment. The hours can be very long, which takes away from my family time." • "Writing grants to support our research is rather time-consuming, and there is no guarantee that the grant will be awarded."

Steps to Current Job

- North Carolina State University in Raleigh, Bachelor of Science in Pre-Med Zoology. Member of the swim team.
- Laboratory technician in the Department of Hematology/Oncology at the University of Virginia in Charlottesville.
- Pennsylvania State University in University Park, Ph.D. in Genetics.
- Postdoctoral fellowship at the National Institute of Environmental Health Sciences in Research Triangle Park, North Carolina.
- Assistant research professor in the Department of Molecular Genetics and Microbiology and Institute of Genome Sciences and Policy; Director of the Duke DNA Microarray Core Facility.

Advice

If you're interested in a career in Holly's field, "pursue a Ph.D. in *Bioinformatics* and Genetics, which includes experience in statistical data analysis and computer programming." Holly also suggests "developing a personality that is not sensitive to criticism and one that can adjust to working with a variety of multidisciplinary groups of people."

"Be assertive, action-oriented, persistent, and open-minded in any task that comes your way in your job. And most importantly, find a job that you love and enjoy."

Helpful Personality Traits

Curious, creative, inquisitive, ambitious, motivated, focused, borderline obsessive, and interested in the field of science and statistics.

Hobbies & Interests

Biking, swimming, and playing with her children and watching them grow.

Genomics is the study of genes and their function.

A *DNA microarray* is a technology tool that captures a "snapshot" of the activity pattern of thousands of genes at once.

Gene expression is a pattern of behavior by a gene.

Bioinformatics is using computer-generated information to analyze biological data.

For more information about Holly's work, go to www.genome.duke.edu/.

EXPERIENCE

Almost every Firestarter said that getting career experience while still in school is important. Volunteering and internships, whether paid or not, allow you to explore a potential career and help you decide whether that career is right for you.

As Kristie Weisner Thompson advises, "Do something besides being a lifeguard every summer. If you want to be a lifeguard one summer then that's fine, but if you really want to figure out what you want to do, maybe be a lifeguard certain days of the week and then spend some time in a real work environment the other days of the week."

You will also make valuable contacts, which helped many of our Firestarters find their first "real" job.

Jane Perlov

Chief of Police for the City of Raleigh, North Carolina

{ *"I very much lead by communicating and consensus. I'm not the queen. I'm the chief."* }

Police Chief Jane Perlov poses with her dog, Astro.

Job Description
Jane oversees all of the "day-to-day" operations (human resources, policies and procedures, equipment, finances, and so on) of her city's police department.

A Day on the Job
Attends daily staff meeting. "I have a staff meeting every morning with my senior staff, both civilians and sworn." • Deals with "the crisis of the day." • Looks at crime statistics. "We're very data-driven here. So I really keep up-to-date on a daily basis as to the crime in the city, any trends and patterns." • Goes out on patrol. "Some days I'll go out on patrol in the afternoon or the evening." • Attends additional meetings. "I meet with community groups to address community concerns and issues. I address Rotary groups, women's

groups, professional organizations. I do a lot of leadership panels." In addition to these types of meetings, other impromptu meetings may arise at her office. For example, she says, "We have a community liaison person, and there may be issues bubbling up in a community that we need to deal with, or there might be training issues. A lot of that comes up during the day. The ultimate decisions are mine." But Jane is quick to point out, "I very much lead by communicating and consensus. I'm not the queen. I'm the chief. That's an important distinction. I'll use the expertise within my organization to help me make decisions." • Determines department's budget. "I make a request to the city manager each year as to what our needs are. Every year the budget goes up by a few million dollars."

Job Likes
"I like that no day is the same." • "I like that every night I go to sleep knowing I affected somebody's life that day. You really have a chance to make a difference in people's lives. It sounds really corny, but it's really true."

Job Challenges
"I have a lot of 'clients.' I have prisoners—bad guys are clients. My community is my client. I deal with elected officials, and I deal with the daily crime issues. So it's balancing all of those balls in the air, and it's a challenge because you're not going to make everybody happy, but my ultimate goal is to keep everybody safe."

Steps to Current Job
- Jane graduated from high school at age 16 and attended New York University, New York City, for two years, working toward a master's in Social Work (MSW). During this time, she worked at a bagel store and sold tickets at Lincoln Theater.
- Fund raiser for the Metropolitan Opera's Patron Program in New York City for two years.
- Lawsuit investigator for New York City's legal department for two years. During this time, Jane took the exams necessary to enter New York's Police Academy. Because New York police officer jobs are in high demand, it took two years before she entered the academy.
- Jane worked in NYC's police department for 18 years in the following positions:
  - Officer for four years.
  - Sergeant for four years.
  - Lieutenant for three years.
  - Captain for one and a half years.
  - Precinct commander on Manhattan's Upper West Side for two years. "I got my own precinct command, which is really what you want. It's what I wanted—to be the captain of my own ship."

- Deputy inspector for one year.
- Inspector for two years.
- Chief of the Queens detective division for one year.
- John Jay College of Criminal Justice, New York, New York; Bachelor of Science in Criminal Justice. Jane worked on this degree while working in New York City's police department.
- Secretary of Public Safety for the Commonwealth of Massachusetts for two and a half years. "This is where networking comes in," says Jane. At a "Women in Government" conference, she met Jane Swift, who at the time was running for the Lieutenant Governor position in Massachusetts. When Swift won the election, she called Jane and offered her the position.
- Chief of Police for the City of Raleigh.

Advice

Jane says if you want to be a police chief, "you have to have a passion for doing it. It's not a job. It's really a calling. It has to be something that you feel inside, that you really can make a commitment to, because it's a very different kind of lifestyle than a lot of other jobs. It's hard to get baby-sitters in the middle of the night if you get called to a homicide scene at three o'clock in the morning." That being said, Jane also says that she tells all of her new women police officers, "you don't have to be one of the boys to be successful. You can be yourself and be really successful at this job."

Jane says, "education is becoming more and more important in police work, certainly as a requirement going up through the ranks. You don't necessarily need a criminal justice degree. I think that the importance of college and police work is that it opens your mind. It shows you things and teaches you about people and cultures and places that you might not have explored."

While you are young and exploring, Jane suggests that you step back before you make a decision, "whether it be driving a car when you're drunk or getting in the car next to a drunk driver or doing drugs or hanging around with people that you shouldn't be hanging around. It's hard to make those decisions, but they're going to be with you the rest of your life."

But Jane doesn't want to underestimate the importance of having a sense of adventure and not being afraid of doing the unexpected. She grew up in an upper-middle-class family of all girls in New York City, and says, "normally in New York City when you become a cop, your father was a cop or your uncle, and there was no such thing in my family. I always had a sense of adventure and always was different. It definitely was out of the ordinary for my family—way out of the ordinary."

Helpful Personality Traits

Have integrity, adventurous, compassionate, passionate, and ethical. "You're put in a lot of positions where you have a lot of tough ethical decisions to make."

Hobbies & Interests

Hiking, nature, bird watching, biking, canoeing, and spending time with her dog.

Janet Green Jacobson

Professional Artist

{ *"You are doing something that completely feeds your soul."* }

Painter Janet Green Jacobson, in her art studio, prepares her color palette.

Job Description

Janet describes a professional artist as someone who attempts to support herself through her artwork. She is a painter whose current subject matter is contemporary landscapes, and her medium is oil on canvas. "My work sort of falls in between traditional and abstract." Janet draws her inspiration from the beauty of her natural surroundings in the mountains of western North Carolina.

A Day on the Job

Goes to her studio, which is separate from her house but on the same property. This provides solitude and keeps her free of distractions. "Being an artist is a very solitary profession. You are alone with yourself and your supplies and your canvas all day long." • Paints five full days a week. "You have to have a lot of self discipline. Anybody who's worked out of their home knows this." Janet usually juggles between five and seven paintings at a time, all in various stages of progress. The average amount of time that she spends on each painting is several weeks. • Markets her artwork. This includes entering shows, showing in galleries or at her studio, photographing the artwork, and maintaining a Web page. Janet also oversees the production and marketing of prints of her artwork. • Running the day-to-day operations of her business, such as accounting, ordering supplies, and so on.

Job Likes

"You are doing something that completely feeds your soul." • "You are your own boss." • "It's been a wonderful career to have while raising kids. Even during the busiest years of raising children, I was always able to continue in my artwork."

Job Challenges

Janet may spend weeks on a painting, only to find "no matter how hard you try, some paintings don't turn out." • Janet would rather spend her time creating than dealing with the business side of showing and selling her artwork. Although it is essential to a professional artist, it's not her favorite duty.

Steps to Current Job

- The University of South Carolina at Columbia; Bachelor of Fine Arts and Master of Fine Arts.
- Graphic artist for an advertising agency for two years.
- Framer in a frame shop for one year.
- Commercial illustrator for two years.
- *Commission* work throughout every stage of her career.
- Artist.

Advice

Janet says that it is important to think of your career as an artist like a journey. "If you looked at my old work and my new work, you'd think it was two different artists. That's part of the growth of an artist." Janet's early artwork focused on Western scenes and her medium was watercolor. Along the way, she responded to changes in her life responsibilities and changed her subject and medium completely. "You have to move on if you're going to be fresh and creative." As with most things, "You have to put your nose to the grindstone and practice and produce." You grow from each piece of artwork, whether or not that piece is successful. Practice allows you not only to get better, but also to develop your own style, and learn tricks and techniques. She points out that creating art is like playing the piano: It simply doesn't come without practice.

Janet quotes Joseph Chilton Pierce: "To live a creative life we must lose our fear of being wrong." Elaborating on that quote, Janet says "I think fear for visual artists is always there. It can be totally paralyzing to paint a picture and put it up on a wall and have a crowd of people look at it. The challenge to any new artist is to conquer that fear and to believe in your artwork and to persevere. If you can conquer that fear, then you're on your way."

As far as careers go, "If you love it, no matter what it is, then you'll find success along the way. If you are able to do what you love, then that in itself is success, in my opinion."

Helpful Personality Traits
Creative, tenacious, thick-skinned, confident in yourself, and "sees the world in a different way."

Hobbies & Interests
Tennis, gardening, and being in the outdoors. "I love hiking, and I think that truly has an influence on my art."

> A *commissioned* art piece is one that an artist is asked to do for a pre-arranged fee. The subject matter is not usually determined by the artist.

Janet's work is displayed at www.wickwireartgallery.com.

Janet Jarriel

Classical Musician Agent

{ *"I'm the 'Jerry Maguire' for opera singers."* }

Job Description
Janet represents opera singers, instrumentalists, and conductors. She handles every aspect of her artists' careers, which includes marketing them, finding venues for them to perform, planning all of their travel arrangements, and

negotiating their contracts. "I am their business liaison." Having an agent allows an artist to concentrate solely on his or her talent.

A Day on the Job

Checks e-mail very early in the morning. "The first thing I do is check my e-mail because I do a lot of international business. Their communication comes during the night." • Attends to pending duties such as returning phone calls, sending head shots and biographies of artists to venues, negotiating contracts, and working on artists' performance schedules and travel arrangements. International communications are attended to immediately. • Speaks with her artists. "I talk to most of my artists on a daily basis." • Markets her artists through promotional e-mail newsletters and postcards, keeping the Web site and artist biographies up-to-date and contacting possible venues. "Updating the Web site is a huge task. I try to keep their schedules up-to-date and their bios all new and fresh." • Travels to view her artists' performances or auditions. This allows Janet to network for her artists and herself and to audition new artists. • Keeps up-to-date on the industry by reading the arts section on www.nytimes.com.

Job Likes

"I am a singer, and so it gives me an opportunity to listen to and work with people that do what I love to hear. I understand it and I love doing it." • "I work with wonderful people. We are not only business partners, but we are friends." • "The other thing I really love, love, love about my job is I can do it from home." Janet has young children, and working from home allows her to spend more time with them and also lets her live in an area of the country that she chooses.

Job Challenges

Sometimes her job can be very stressful. "At any moment an artist can say, 'I've decided to go with a different agency,' and you put a lot of time and money into an artist." Having to deal with situations that arise during her artists' travels can also be stressful. For example, when an artist is in another country and part of their prearranged schedule or their negotiations doesn't happen as planned, it is stressful to fix the problem immediately from so far away. • In this industry, dealing with temperaments is challenging. Budgets are tight, and jobs are high stress. For these reasons, Janet finds that working with people in music can sometimes be difficult. • "It is difficult to 'break into' this job." Most musicians' agents live in New York, Los Angeles, or other large cities.

Steps to Current Job

- Mercer University in Macon, Georgia; Bachelor of Arts in Music with a concentration in voice.

- Soprano soloist, administrative staff, and children's choir director for a church in Florida for two years.
- Director of marketing working her way into television producer for an international television series called *The Joy of Music* for three years.
- Indiana University in Bloomington; Master of Arts Administration. Worked for the school of music admissions office.
- Started an agency for classical musicians.

Advice

It is essential that you study in the field you want to represent. "Study music so that you have a good working knowledge of repertoire and you understand music." Other areas that are helpful in this career are classes in law, business marketing, accounting, and international business. "And if you at all can, speak another language: Italian, French, or German." Although it is not required, knowing another language is respected and can open many doors. In the classical music business, Italian is probably the most useful language to learn. Janet also emphasizes the importance of learning to play the piano.

Janet believes it is important to have a "rock-solid self esteem," and this can be achieved by having a solid faith and spiritual foundation. It is also important to know that you are special, and that you can do anything you want, but that it will take hard work and sacrifice.

Helpful Personality Traits

Organized, good at multitasking, good memory, businesslike attitude because it is easy to get emotionally involved, hardworking, and compassionate.

Hobbies & Interests

Music of all kinds, her children, church, and travel.

For more information about Janet and her work, see www.jejartists.com.

"Carpe Diem"

—Latin for "Seize the Day"

Joan Lamson

Mayor of Pine Knoll Shores, North Carolina

{ *"Town government is business. You've got revenues and you've got expenses, you've got to figure out where the money's going to come from and how you're going to finance things."* }

Job Description
Joan is an elected official and "primary spokesperson" for her town, Pine Knoll Shores. In Joan's town, there is a mayor-council form of government. This means that the mayor and town council are the employers of the town's staff, and people report to them. In a council-manager form of government, the staff reports to the manager, and the mayor is more of a figurehead.

A Day on the Job
Works from home until about 10:00 a.m. • Checks in with town administrator, "to see if there's anything that she's got that I need to know about." • Goes through her in-box to see what needs immediate attention. • Checks on projects. "I try to move each project along a little bit." An example of a project that Joan is working on is getting federal money for beach nourishment. In order to do this, the town has to secure public access to the beaches from private beach-property owners. • Talks with citizens or commissioners about concerns or projects. "My office is at the very front of the building, so people often just poke their head in and sit and talk." • Signs official papers of the town: minutes of meetings, contracts, and so on. • Checks in with department heads (police chief, fire chief, and so on) to "see how things are going in their departments. I feel like it's really important to stay in touch with the employees." • Answers any phone messages.

Job Likes
"Oh, I love my job!" • "I like the work. I like the kinds of projects that come before me." • "I like being asked for an opinion." • "I like complex problems. I like putting pieces together and seeing how things can work. I like creating solutions where it seems like no one loses too much." • "This is the most fun I've had since I sold my business!"

Job Challenges

Joan works with a group of commissioners and finds, "Trying to get people to work as a team when they come from very, very different philosophies and different backgrounds—that's the real challenge for me."

Steps to Current Job

- Classes at University of Denver, Colorado. Joan got married shortly after starting school and became the mother of three children.
- Stayed at home with her children while they were young.
- Switchboard operator/receptionist, promoted to inside salesperson. Joan worked for the company for a total of seven years.
- Product manager in outside sales department for 10 months.
- Outside sales for five years while working on her MBA.
- Case Western Reserve University, Weatherhead School of Management, Cleveland, Ohio; Master of Business Administration. This university offered a special program for women in management. Joan explains, "If you had 10 years' work experience, you could get into it. It was a special kind of certificate, and if you completed that, you could get into the MBA program."
- Sales manager for less than one year.
- Business owner of a metal-finishing company for 20 years.
- Sold her business. Served on the board of her local Chamber of Commerce and became a volunteer for Service Corps of Retired Executives (SCORE). SCORE is sponsored by the U.S. Small Business Administration, and Joan explains, "It's volunteers who have been in business and who counsel people who want to start businesses."
- Mayor of Pine Knoll Shores.

Advice

Joan says, "Pay attention to world issues and understand how governments work." She also thinks the earlier you become involved in politics of some sort, the better—"either precinct politics or just helping 'get out the vote.'" A degree in political science would be ideal, and Joan said that getting a fellowship to the Institute of Political Leadership has helped prepare her for her role as mayor. She also thinks that her MBA has been very helpful. "Town government is business. You've got revenues and you've got expenses, you've got to figure out where the money's going to come from and how you're going to finance things."

"The strongest advice that I have for any woman is prepare to support yourself. That doesn't mean that I'm advocating the absence of marriage." Joan goes on to say that supporting yourself might even make you a better marriage partner. "You could be a much more interesting person to talk to because you normally have a variety of experiences [when you work]."

Helpful Personality Traits

Team player, diplomatic, gregarious—"being able to speak to people you don't know," and good with follow-through: "If you're going to make a promise, you need to follow through."

Hobbies & Interests

Cooking, eating out with friends, reading, working on the computer, movies, and travel.

Jodi Schwartz

Multimedia Production Company Owner/Executive Producer

{ *"There's a deep satisfaction of knowing that you're providing livelihood for 17 other human beings."* }

Executive producer and business owner Jodi Schwartz follows up on a script revision for a corporate video.

Job Description

As a business owner, Jodi manages the day-to-day operations necessary to run her company and is always looking for new ways to service existing clients. In conjunction with this role, her job as executive producer has her overseeing many clients' projects with her company.

A Day on the Job

Executive Producer

Interacts with client by e-mail or phone. • Determines the best group of people to work on a particular project (producer, writer, graphic artist/programmer, editor). • Manages the team to make sure that the client is satisfied, deadlines are being met, and the project is within budget.

Business Owner

Oversees accounting of the business using accounting software—"QuickBooks® is a big part of the accounting side of running the business." • Deals with many human resource (employee) issues, such as insurance, vacation, compensation, and discipline. • Looks for ways to expand her company's role for existing clients. "I'm constantly telling them about things that we're doing with other clients and trying to expand our role with them."

Job Likes

"I have to say a big part of what I like about my job is the client interaction, and as the company has developed, looking at the work when it's done is a big satisfaction." • As a business owner, Jodi says, "There's a deep satisfaction of knowing that you're providing livelihood for 17 other human beings. A big reason for maintaining and continuing to grow is knowing that you're providing a home or a place for people to call home in their work."

Job Challenges

Jodi says, "A lot of my day is not creative—not to say I don't see the creative and maybe get a say in it, but I'm no longer editing like I used to." • "From a business owner standpoint, it's volatile. Wow, if there's a dip in the economy that affects our business, it's not just me… there are other people involved."

Steps to Current Job

- State University of New York at Albany; Bachelor of Science in Macro-economics.
- When she was preparing to graduate, Jodi realized, "I really like studying economics, but I don't want to go out and practice it. So now what do I do?" She ended up taking an unpaid internship with a top video editor for a few months.

- Editorial assistant for 12 months with the same edit facility where she had interned.
- Video editor/producer for four years, both freelance and full-time.
- Business owner/editor/executive producer.

Advice

Jodi says that you can never be too detail-oriented or organized to be a good producer. Learning to delegate is also important because "you're not doing the actual work, so you want to make sure that you're assembling the right team." She also thinks that "internships are great. Be a PA (production assistant) on shoots." If you're planning on starting your own business, you want to find a partner... not to do it all by yourself because that's really hard."

"Be true to yourself and be honest about what you want to do. I go back to businesses where I like people and I like what they stand for. So if you're true to yourself... I think people are going to come back to you because they want to do business with you." Another piece of advice Jodi gives is, "Never burn bridges because every person you deal with, no matter where they are or what the situation is, they could always come back and be a prospective employer, client, or employee."

Jodi thinks that it's important to be realistic, "You don't want to do something that you enjoy, but it doesn't provide you a lifestyle you want to live, because then you're unbalanced." For example, if you want to live in a major city, you'll probably need to have a career that will pay for the higher cost of living.

Helpful Personality Traits

Ambition and drive, because owning your own business is an "uphill battle"; detail oriented and organized.

Hobbies & Interests

Spending time with her children, boating, working out, fine dining, and socializing with friends.

Johnna Watson

Associate Dean of Enrollment Management and Information Systems for a Graduate School

{ *"I like that it serves a really good purpose."* }

Job Description

Johnna's job is to recruit, admit, and enroll students to the more than 98 graduate programs at the university. She is also responsible for marketing the graduate programs to various audiences, using a variety of electronic and print media. Much of her work revolves around developing and enhancing databases to store electronic data, such as biographical and demographic information as well as academic history and technical support information.

A Day on the Job

Supervises a staff of 11 people. • Manages the admissions and information systems operations of the office. • Communicates with prospective students via surface mail, e-mail, and telephone. • Counsels students about the university's 98-plus graduate programs and about careers in various fields. • Works on the computer a lot. "Probably 85 percent of what I do is with the computer." • Liaisons with faculty and staff in numerous offices on campus to facilitate the admission and enrollment of graduate students. • Works with staff in the Information Technology Systems department to develop, test, deploy, maintain, and enhance its Student Information System (SIS).

Job Likes

"I like the variety. I like that it's always challenging." • Johnna enjoys the freedom her job entails. "I like that I have a lot of autonomy with what I do." • "I like that it serves a really good purpose. It helps people who want to return to school gain the skills they need to pursue a particular career choice." • "The supervision is the most difficult part, but it's also one of the most rewarding because it's an opportunity to interact with people on a real personal level. It's nice to be in a position to encourage other people's growth."

Job Challenges

"There's too much to do." Because the university where Johnna works is rapidly growing, "It's really difficult to stay on top of everything the graduate school needs to do in order to support the graduate faculty, staff, and students."

Steps to Current Job

- Peace College in Raleigh, North Carolina; Associate degree in Liberal Arts.
- University of North Carolina at Pembroke; Bachelor of Arts in Communication Studies with a concentration in Journalism.
- Admissions counselor for four years.
- Assistant director of undergraduate admissions for three years.
- University of North Carolina at Charlotte, Master of Arts in Counseling. Johnna earned this degree while working full time.

- Associate director of undergraduate admissions for two years.
- Assistant dean of enrollment management and information systems for the graduate school for six years.
- University of North Carolina at Charlotte; Doctorate in Curriculum and Instruction—in progress.
- Associate Dean of enrollment management and information systems for the graduate school.

Advice

Johnna would encourage anyone interested in a career in university admissions to "connect with their admissions office while they're an undergraduate student and volunteer to be a student tour guide or an ambassador—to get connected with the university in some administrative way." A master's degree is usually required of jobs like Johnna's, and a doctoral degree is often preferred; so plan to pursue some type of post-baccalaureate degree.

"Talk to a lot of people about what they do to have a good idea of some of the real, relevant jobs that are available… so your path can be more purposeful." Once you narrow down your career-search selections, Johnna says, "try and get part-time jobs in those fields, just to be exposed to what the field is like."

"Have a good friend and support system. I just think it helps to have some-body, even if it's just one person, to confide in, in order to brainstorm and put life in perspective."

Helpful Personality Traits

Outgoing, organized, high tolerance for stress*, and able to juggle multiple projects.

Hobbies & Interests

Spending time with family, reading, and cooking

---

*"Educational institutions, whether they're public or private, are driven by headcount. How many students are enrolled? How many classes did they take, and *pay* for? If we don't have enough students, we can't pay our faculty. We can't pay our light bill. I'm held accountable if our enrollment is not where it needs to be."

Joyce Beatty

Director of Counseling, Testing, and Career Placement Center for a Community College (Retired)

{ *"We help people solve problems... we don't give advice."* }

Job Description

As you can see from her title, Joyce's department had many functions, and she made sure that they all ran smoothly. Ultimately, Joyce was responsible for making sure every enrolling student was tested to determine where they should be placed academically, that any counseling crises were handled properly, and that all graduating students went through career placement activities. In addition, she made sure that the college was following accessibility codes spelled out in the Americans with Disabilities Act (ADA) and that all students with documented disabilities were accommodated according to their individual needs.

A Day on the Job

Coordinated activities in the Counseling, Testing, and Career Placement Center. • Supervised a secretary and counselor. • Made sure that placement tests were administered to all incoming freshmen. • Interpreted student placement tests to determine entering students' skills. • Talked with students about their goals and test results. • Handled any crisis that might arise with students or faculty. • Counseled students about personal, academic, or career issues. • Represented the college on several community committees. • Set objectives and goals for her department and made sure they were met. • Filed reports to ensure accreditation. • Taught a psychology course each semester. Joyce was not required to teach, but felt that it gave her an appreciation of both students' and teachers' positions.

Job Likes

"I really liked the student contact." • "It was really rewarding to see the students' accomplishments." • "I did research, and I enjoyed doing that." She would keep lists and reports and identify trends by running statistical analysis on test results. • Teaching was an optional part of Joyce's job that she really appreciated.

Job Challenges

"The politics involved was the biggest thing that I disliked about my job." • The paperwork could sometimes seem daunting to Joyce. "I didn't like all of the reporting."

Steps to Current Job

Joyce had no college education prior to her first husband's death. "After he died, I realized that I needed to have more education to help me support myself and the two kids."

- University of North Carolina at Pembroke; Bachelor of Science in Psychology.
- East Carolina University in Greenville, North Carolina; master's in Counseling.
- Nova Southeastern in Fort Lauderdale, Florida; Doctorate in Higher Education.
- High school counselor for six months.
- Community college. Joyce started as a counselor and worked her way up to her final position as director of counseling, testing, and career placement.

Advice

Joyce says, "You have to want to help people solve problems. One of the biggest misconceptions about being a counselor is that counselors give advice. We help people solve problems. We don't give advice." She goes on to explain that the community college system requires counselors to have a master's degree in counseling. "You cannot have *any* master's degree; it has to be in counseling." In addition to the master's degree, state and national certifications are available. Joyce was licensed as a counselor at the state level and also as a National Certified Counselor. "I would advise anybody to sit for the additional exams because the additional certification gives more credibility to the profession."

Joyce gave this advice to her own children and thinks that it is even more important today. "Every semester that you're in high school, take math and science because you can't get too much, and you want to leave your options open." She explains that you might not think that you want to be in a field that uses math or science when you head to college, but if you change your mind and don't have that background, it's harder to make up for the deficit.

Helpful Personality Traits

Outgoing, good at statistics, even-tempered, approachable, easy to talk with, non-judgmental, empathetic, and nurturing.

Hobbies & Interests

Playing bridge, being with people, cooking, entertaining, gardening, reading anything and everything, keeping up with the news, and painting.

Juli Kim

Research and Policy Associate

{ *"My job is a lot like being a reporter, teacher, and facilitator."* }

Job Description
Juli is an attorney who works for a state commission that developed the state's current corrections sentencing policy. This commission's responsibilities include advising the state legislature on changes to sentencing options within the criminal and juvenile justice systems.

A Day on the Job
Researches current issues related to sentencing of adult and juvenile offenders. • Meets with juvenile and adult correction administrators, court officials, and legislative staff to discuss issues relevant to adult and juvenile sentencing policy. • Meets with co-workers to determine how to present their findings to the commission at quarterly meetings. • Presents findings to the commission.

Job Likes
Juli likes being up-to-date about policy issues within the justice system and knowing that the research and analysis she provides often have an immediate impact. • She also enjoys knowing how state legislature works and being "in the know."

Job Challenges
The politics and the manipulation of the process are frustrating. A lot of times she feels, "it's hard to accomplish anything because of the bureaucracy."

Steps to Current Job
- University of North Carolina at Chapel Hill, Bachelor of Science in Psychology.
- UNC-Chapel Hill Law School, Juris Doctorate.
- Delinquency attorney for three years.
- Middle-school teacher for one year.
- Research and policy associate.

Advice

Juli thinks that it is really important to know as much as possible about policy issues and how government policy is made. She suggests that women interested in this career definitely get a job within the government to understand how it works.

"It's really important that young women start thinking about and exploring their interests early on." She thinks that exploration is especially important because a lot of times young people pattern themselves on their parents. By exploring, Juli believes that you can have a better understanding of what makes you happy. She also feels that young women should consider what kind of life they want outside of their career. If having a family is important to you, think about how career and children will mix.

Helpful Personality Traits

Curious, analytical, flexible, and able to communicate well.

Hobbies & Interests

Cooking, running, reading, and spending time with her kids.

Julia Brooks

Interior Designer, IIDA, Business Owner

{ *"It's almost like a scavenger hunt."* }

Job Description

Based on the functional needs a client has for a space and through a step-by-step process, an interior designer creates a functional, yet aesthetically pleasing space. The majority of Julia's work is designing and furnishing model homes for builders across the country.

A Day on the Job

Checks e-mail and returns all phone calls. "From 8:30 [a.m.] to 12:30 [p.m.], I'm pretty much on the phone because there are so many contacts that you have to make." • Goes to client's space to take measurements (if necessary) and designs plans for homeowner or builder. • Creates budgets and timelines. • Prepares presentations to explain design to client. • Goes on buying trips to purchase furnishings and finishes (fabrics, wall coverings, and paints) for her design projects. "We are in *High Point* [NC], or someplace, and we're going from showroom to showroom to purchase." • Places orders and checks on the price and inventory of items she wishes to purchase. "Just because we select it doesn't mean that it's going to be the right price, it's going to be available in the time frame we need. These are things that we have to check out." • Checks with her company's warehouse to make sure that deliveries have been made. • Supervises drapery workers and installers, artists, and anyone else who has a hand in bringing Julia's designs to life. • Markets herself and her company.

Job Likes
"I love the freedom and the flexibility of designing… not having to be held within the box." • "It's almost like a scavenger hunt… things that you find that you can put together and come up with some end product that is something totally different from what you originally thought." • "You're not doing the same thing every day, and that every day is so different that you can't be bored—never would you be bored." • "I just have a passion for it."

Job Challenges
"Paperwork… the day-to-day aspects of your business. Not only do you have to be a good designer, but you need to be a good businessperson. That's something that I'm always working on."

Steps to Current Job
- East Carolina University in Greenville, North Carolina; Bachelor of Science in Interior Design and some graduate work in design.
- Interior designer for a firm for two years.
- President and owner of an interior design firm.

Advice
Julia says that if you're interested in a career in interior design, you should, "take any and every art course that you can with some emphasis on architectural drafting." If possible, take some construction management courses. Julia says they will help you tremendously because, "you've got to learn the building, you've got to learn the codes, you've got to learn that aspect of design as well." She also thinks that business, marketing, and accounting courses will be very helpful if you want to work for yourself.

"Interior design can encompass a wide range of requirements and aspects of design, so… you have to decide what aspect you want to do—whether you want to work with people with their homes, or if you want to work with businesses… doing banks or hospitals."

"Take a certain aspect of your life that you love… and build upon it through the years."

Helpful Personality Traits

People person, positive attitude, and communicative.

Hobbies & Interests

Jogging, music (serves on the North Carolina Opera Membership Committee), swimming, watching football and basketball.

IIDA (International Interior Design Association) is a professional association/certification for interior designers. In order to receive this certification, a designer has to have been a designer a specific amount of time and pass a written exam as well as a drawing exam. Julia equates it to the certification that a Certified Public Accountant receives.

High Point, North Carolina, is considered by many in Julia's field to be the "furniture capital" of the world. Twice a year, furniture manufacturers and dealers display their new lines to the trade (designers, furniture-store buyers, and so on).

Kathleen Boykin

Family Nurse Practitioner

{ *"I really like getting to know the people in my community."* }

Job Description

Kathleen provides primary medical care to patients at a family medical practice. She works mostly with basic health problems and the wellness of her patients. The difference between Kathleen and the doctor at the family practice is their level of responsibility. Kathleen is not required to be on call or make hospital rounds, and she is not personally liable in the event of a malpractice suit. In her state she is allowed to prescribe medications, but each state has different rules and regulations concerning nurse practitioners' responsibilities.

A Day on the Job
Reviews patient lab work and calls the patient if results are abnormal. • Sees patients every 15 minutes from 8:00 a.m. to 12:30 p.m. • Takes a 30-minute lunch break. • Sees patients until 3:00 p.m.

Job Likes
"I enjoy helping others." Kathleen says that she knows it sounds cliché, but that's why she really likes her job. She feels that a nursing background helps her to be a more well-rounded caregiver because she looks at the person as a whole, not as just a health problem. • Kathleen's schedule works well with her lifestyle. She is able to arrange her schedule so that she can be home when her children get out of school. Because she's not on call and making hospital rounds, Kathleen likes that her job does not take her away from home on evenings and weekends. • "I really like getting to know the people in my community." Kathleen enjoys seeing her patients when she is out and about.

Job Challenges
"The way the health-care system is going, we're getting reimbursed less and less, and so now in order to make a business prosperous, we have to try and see as many patients as we can." Having a strict 15-minute schedule with each patient and seeing a large quantity of patients can be stressful.

Steps to Current Job
- University of North Carolina at Chapel Hill, Bachelor of Science in Nursing (BSN).
- Medical/surgical nurse for a hospital for two years.
- Occupational health nurse for a company for two years.
- University of North Carolina at Chapel Hill, Master of Science of Nursing (Family Nurse Practitioner program; MSN).
- Family nurse practitioner at a family practice.

Advice
Kathleen suggests pursuing a BSN, rather than an associate degree, if you want to ultimately be a nurse practitioner. You will eventually have to get a BSN before entering a nurse-practitioner program, so you might as well already have it. She also feels that after receiving your BSN, you should work for at least four years as a nurse before going for your MSN. You are required to work for only one year before starting a master's program, but she believes that you build a "better knowledge base" with more nursing experience under your belt. And while working as a nurse, Kathleen says, "I would recommend hospital nursing to get the most experience."

"I'm telling my daughters to figure out their highest priority before college." Once you decide your highest priority, pick a career that can work around it or with it. If your highest priority is to have a family, choose something that will allow a flexible schedule.

Helpful Personality Traits
Caring, independent, intelligent, and personable.

Hobbies & Interests
Running, triathlons, water activities, outdoor activities, and politics.

DON'T LET THE AMOUNT OF SCHOOL REQUIRED TURN YOU OFF FROM A JOB

You shouldn't decide against a career because it requires a lot of school. An additional four to six years might seem like a lot right now, but in the scheme of things, four to six years out of a possible 40-year working career is not that much.

If you feel like you can't afford to go to school, there are loans, grants, and scholarships that can help lighten the financial burden. Our Firestarters had the same concerns when they were contemplating higher education. Find out about Tonya Baker, a pharmacist, on page 226. While attending a state university, she took some of her classes at a community college to save money. On page 175, you'll read about Maria Kelly-Doggett, a chemical engineer who participated in a co-op program that allowed her go to school a semester, then work a semester in engineering. Not only was she making money for school, but she was building up her resume. Many colleges offer jobs on campus, and it's understood that school comes first and the jobs will accommodate your schedule. Most high schools have career centers where you can go for more guidance on affording college. If you're in college, check with your financial aid office.

Starting your journey takes one day at a time. You will be so much happier and fulfilled doing something that truly interests you.

And remember, along your journey, you will not be alone. There will be many others on the same educational path as you. You will meet many interesting people who share your interests and intellect. You will form lifetime friends and relationships during this time in your life.

Kathryn Millican

Manager of Public Policy Development for a Health Insurance Company

{ *"I take a term paper and turn it into a bumper sticker."* }

Job Description

Kathryn reviews state legislation to determine how it will impact her company. She determines the company's position on the bill and then puts it into simple language or *talking points* that the company's lobbyist can use when speaking with state senators and representatives (legislators).

A Day on the Job

Reviews legislative updates to determine whether any bills have been introduced that might affect her company. • Reads legislation to determine what areas of her company will be impacted if it passes. • Leads her company's Legislative Advisory Group (LAG). The LAG is a cross-functional team that represents different areas of the company. As a group, they review legislation and determine how to make the legislation have less of an impact on the company. • Determines her company's position on a particular bill and shares this information with the government affairs vice president and company lobbyist. Kathryn then provides them with written analysis of the recommended position and arguments that they can share with legislators. She also gives them compromise language to use if it becomes evident that their position will not be approved by the legislature. • Checks the calendars for the state senate, house of representatives, and individual committees to see when they will be in session and what bills will be considered. • Talks with lobbyists about what bills are up for discussion that concern the company and goes over main talking points. • Makes contacts with other parties that are affected by the legislation, such as the hospital association, the medical society, the department of insurance, and other health insurance companies. • Participates in legislative sessions.

Job Likes

Kathryn loves the independence of her job. She has a "hands-off" manager and finds it empowering that he doesn't micromanage, but Kathryn knows that "he's there if I need him." • "What may be true in the morning may not be true at lunch and is completely different at the end of the day." • There is a lot of skill involved in Kathryn's job. She is often drafting legislation and has to come up with the best way to write it so that people can't find ways to "poke holes" in it. • "I want to know everything, and you have to have that personal connection to know what's going on. The media cannot be your only source of information." • Because legislation can affect any department within the company, Kathryn gets to see how every group in her company operates. She likes that she doesn't work with the same group of people everyday.

Job Challenges

Kathryn is hard pressed to find anything she dislikes about her job. Even the fact that she might work for long periods of time on something that never "sees the light of day" doesn't bother her. She knows that her work might have kept a bill with negative consequences for her company from passing.

Steps to Current Job

- Furman University, Greenville, South Carolina; Bachelor of Arts in Political Science.
- Clerk for the North Carolina senate for 18 months.
- Executive director for the Governor's Task Force for Driving While Impaired for one year.
- Special assistant to the chief of staff for North Carolina's lieutenant governor for two years.
- Health care analyst for State Capital Strategies—A Washington Post Company—for two years.
- Managed care analyst for her current company for 18 months.
- University of North Carolina at Chapel Hill, Master of Science in Healthcare Administration. Kathryn worked on this degree while at her current job.
- Manager of public policy development.

Advice

Kathryn says that anyone going into public policy needs to learn the legislative process. "You can't learn by reading about it. You have to experience it." She suggests that you do an internship with your state legislature. Kathryn also suggests that you have a general understanding of the industry for which you plan to work.

"Get out there and try different things," is Kathryn's biggest piece of advice. She says that nothing just comes to you, so don't be afraid to go for what you want. "Nothing is forever. If you get into a job that is not a good fit, you are not stuck in that job forever. Determine what you like and dislike about the job and create an appropriate exit strategy. A job that is better suited for you is out there."

Kathryn also says to realize that "school opens doors, but experience is equally important."

Helpful Personality Traits
Extreme attention to detail, adaptable to change, independent, self motivated, critical thinker, and intellectual.

Hobbies & Interests
Reading, live sporting events (basketball, football, baseball), volunteering, and being active with her husband (walking, cycling, basketball, working out).

> *Talking points* are brief, easy-to-understand verbal summarizations of complex issues.

Kayla Holden

Tax Accounting Manager and Accounting Software Advisor

{ *"I would have thought that CPAs would sit behind their desks all day... and kind of be a geek in the corner."* }

Job Description
Kayla is a *Certified Public Accountant (CPA)* for a *public accounting firm*. In one of her roles, as tax accounting manager, she manages financial records for businesses and individuals. Financial records may include bank reconciliations, income statements, general ledgers, balance sheets, and tax returns. She and her staff prepare and review these statements and ensure that deadlines for filing them are met. She also advises her clients based on their financial performance and about tax laws.

Kayla's other role as accounting software advisor involves working with small-business clients that do not have an accountant on staff. She helps them with the accounting software installation and trains them on the proper use of it. Kayla reviews these clients' financial statements throughout the year to check for accuracy and to offer advice. Many times, she prepares their tax returns.

A Day on the Job

Meets with clients to review their financial records. • Prepares tax returns. • Reviews tax returns completed by her staff. • Delivers tax returns to the client—"kind of an exit conference [a meeting with a client that wraps up the project and keeps communication open for future projects]." • Fields questions from clients about tax laws and tax-law changes. • Works at a client's place of business. "Working with either their office manager or their bookkeeper/accountant, looking at their financial records. I probably spend 40 percent of my time out of the office."

Job Likes

Kayla enjoys her job's flexibility. "We set our own schedules, and we make our own appointments. I can work from home. I can take the afternoon off. I could work at night or Saturdays. As long as we meet with our clients and we can service the clients and meet our billable goals, then we have flexibility to arrange our schedule anyway we need to." • "I like the continual change." Whether it's dealing with different clients or staying up-to-date on tax-law changes, she enjoys that her job is never stagnant. "I love working with different clients. You never get bored, you never know what to expect. It's always a challenge. I'm always learning and always going to classes."

Job Challenges

"The challenge for me is to balance my family and my work. That's a personal challenge because I have a seven-year-old daughter, and she's my top priority. But then there are times that work has to be a top priority. When it is tax season [January 1 through April 15], and it's the busy season as we call it... it's hard to find that balance."

Steps to Current Job

- Mars Hill College, Mars Hill, North Carolina; Bachelor of Science in Accounting, minor in Business Administration, and a concentration in Marketing and Management. Kayla earned college credit for an internship she did one semester.
- Auditor for a public accounting firm for one and a half years.
- Assistant *controller* for a real estate developer for two years.
- Auditor and tax accountant for a small public accounting firm for two years. Took an intense review class for three months and earned her Certified Public Accountant title.
- Took time off while her daughter was an infant, and consulted part-time.
- Tax staff accountant for a public accounting firm. She has worked her way up to her present positions as tax accounting manager and accounting software advisor.

Advice

"The biggest advice that I could give, while a student, is to get work experience." Kayla worked as an intern for an accounting firm during one tax season. She earned college credit, but did not get paid for her help. "That experience gave me the foot in that I needed to get my first job." Kayla also suggests talking with a counselor about career possibilities and to take personality tests that help you figure out what you are best suited to do. "You're making a lifelong decision and it's sometimes at a point in your life when you really don't know what you want to be."

"I think it would be wise to put your goals down on paper." Kayla advises readers to look at their lives as a total picture and see where their job fits in. "Parents can try to really influence their kids... and I think it's good to listen to your parents because they have your best interest in mind; but you have to do what's going to make you happy."

Helpful Personality Traits

A people person, outgoing, confident in yourself and your ability, analytical, and pays close attention to detail.

Hobbies & Interests

Shopping, golf, traveling, snow skiing, spending time with family, and volunteering with her daughter's activities.

Certified Public Accountant (CPA): "It distinguishes you from other accountants. It means that you've completed the required education... obtained a degree, and that you have passed a standardized test.... You're held accountable for your actions.... We are set to a higher standard."

A *controller* works for a company and prepares the financial statements for it.

A *public accounting firm* provides accounting services to businesses or individuals. The public accountants in the firm deal with many issues including tax, audit, consulting, and accounting. To learn more about the different fields of accounting, go to the Occupational Outlook Handbook on the U.S. Department of Labor's Web site: www.bls.gov.

Kelly Carew

Camp Program Director

{ *"I like getting to teach college students how to be good counselors and to provide that experience to them because I feel like they grow so much just as people."* }

Job Description

Kelly is the staff recruiter and staff trainer for a girls' camp in the mountains of western North Carolina. During the summer, she is in charge of training and managing the camp counselors. She is also responsible for coordinating camp activities, such as campouts, water-skiing, tennis, gymnastics, assemblies, and so on. In the winter months, Kelly visits college campuses to recruit and hire camp counselors for the next season.

A Day on the Job

Summer

Attends a morning staff meeting to discuss problems and prepare for the day. • Oversees the morning assembly for the entire camp and makes any special announcements. • Manages sections of the Web site. • Returns phone calls to parents. • Makes preparations for afternoon activities. • Checks on campers and counselors following afternoon activities. • Makes preparations for the next day's activities. • Plans the evening program and lets the counselors set it up and present it. • Listens and supports counselors and answers any of their questions or concerns. • Does counselors' jobs on their days off.

Pre-Fall

Winds up the summer—"a lot of paperwork and surveys." • Plans recruiting trips to colleges.

Fall

Visits colleges. • Assesses the previous summer.

Winter/Spring

Completes the hiring process to be certain all counselor spots are filled. • Prepares for summer.

Job Likes
"I'm a variety person. I like a lot of changes." • Kelly likes working with children, and her job allows her interaction with the campers. • "I like getting to teach college students how to be good counselors and to provide that experience to them because I feel like they grow so much just as people."

Job Challenges
"Camp is a very big commitment, personally. I give up my summers." During the summers, Kelly lives at the camp and does not get to socialize with people outside it. • People tend to glorify Kelly's recruiting trips to college towns. She explains that she is not there to party or play; she's working. Although the travel is interesting it can also be draining, and it takes her away from her personal life.

Steps to Current Job
- University of North Florida in Jacksonville; Bachelor of Arts in Elementary Physical Education. Worked as a camp counselor at Camp Greystone during the summer.
- Worked in a retail specialty shop for two years while waiting for a job to open at Camp Greystone.
- Program director for Camp Greystone.

Advice
You gain experience by attending different camps. She suggests working at other camps while waiting for an opening at the camp where you want to work. This allows you to gain more camp experience and to learn different approaches to camp programs.

Some of Kelly's advice is to "do what you like" and "surround yourself with people that you respect." She also says to strive to maintain the character that you want to have at all times. Don't compromise your principles.

Helpful Personality Traits
Confident, nurturing, empathetic, energetic, enjoy working with all kinds of people, and a desire to help others.

Hobbies & Interests
Being active, running, team sports, and having fun.

Kelly Hopkin

Technical Support for Fabric-Design Software

{ *"I'm on the edge of the creative part of it, but the specifics of what my job entails just fit my personality a lot better."* }

Job Description

Kelly works for a company that creates and sells a graphic-design software package used by textile designers and manufacturers. The designers use the software to help them design fabric and prepare their designs for weaving. She provides technical support to customers and is responsible for helping them with the installation, training, and daily functions of the software.

A Day on the Job

Checks e-mails and handles the most critical problems immediately. • Provides technical support to customers. "The majority of my day is working with customers." • Calls software programmers at the main office in Germany when she needs technical support and to discuss the software functionality. She usually makes these calls before noon because of the time difference. "There's a lot of back-and-forth with them about development, things that aren't working right, suggestions or ideas that either come from me or our clients." • Tracks and contacts customers who need to update their software leases. • Communicates about project details with her U.S. co-workers mostly via the phone and e-mail. • Travels to the main office in Germany for meetings. • Visits clients. "Usually I can handle things over the phone. I can get into their systems and check, delete, update, or fix things. Sometimes that doesn't work. Sometimes there's a hardware or network problem that I can't fix over the phone or via the modem." • Translates the software-tool tips and documentation from German into English. The software is distributed worldwide.

Job Likes

"I like the flexibility of it because I can basically do whatever I want. And, as long as my clients are happy, my boss is happy. I really like that. I don't like people looking over my shoulder and checking every single thing I do." Kelly works from home and finds this flexibility very helpful with having a family. • "I like the people I work with a lot. It's mostly young, smart, computer-literate people from the U.S. and Europe." She has worked with some of them for 10 years and considers them her friends. • "I'm on the edge of the creative part of it, but the specifics of what my job entails just fit my personality a lot better." • "I get to , interact with the customers, train them, and travel with them, and I like that."

Job Challenges

It's a small company, in a small niche, so Kelly finds that "there is not a lot of upward mobility or potential change in my position." But, she also says that she's not interested in "climbing the corporate ladder." • Because the company is small, it does not offer many fringe benefits such as stock options and retirement savings plans that a larger company might.

Steps to Current Job

- North Carolina State University in Raleigh; Bachelor of Science in Textile Science with a concentration in Textile Design; minor in French and Business; member of the soccer team.
- Textile designer for a textile company for one year. She discovered she enjoyed the computer side of her job more than design.
- Customer support for a design software company for three years.
- Product development assistant for a textile manufacturing company for six months.
- Freelance textile design consultant for one year.
- Technical Support Manager for the design software company where she previously worked in customer support.

Advice

"I think it would have been helpful to me if I had taken some more computer design and graphics classes in school. Because I didn't do a lot of computer stuff in college, I didn't realize that I was good at it. In the '80s, art and computer technology weren't totally integrated yet; and if they had been, I think I would have realized that's where I needed to be." Kelly points out that the integration of art and computer technology opens up many new opportunities for young people today.

"I think it's important to really, really think about what you're interested in as a job. It's important to actually try and imagine yourself doing something day after day. Think of the types of things you like to do and see how they would translate into a job. You have to identify, as early as you can, what your strengths and weaknesses are and be honest about them." When Kelly was offered a sales job with her company, she declined because she says "I'm not that type of person. I do better with the more technical end of it; figuring out problems. In general, you have to figure out what type of personality you have and how that would translate into a job you would like."

Helpful Personality Traits

Interested in computers, art, and math; adaptability to quickly changing situations; good judgment; and organizational skills.

Hobbies & Interests

Soccer, crafts, beading, playing with her children, being outdoors, coaching, and crossword puzzles.

Kirstie Tice Spadie

Artistic Director, Owner, and Dance Teacher for the North Carolina Dance Institute

{ *"Your friends are not going to walk through the Broadway stage door with you, so you cannot think like your friends think."* }

Dance teacher Kirstie Tice Spadie in her role as Victoria, the White Cat, in the national tour of *Cats*.

Job Description

Kirstie owns a dance studio, the North Carolina Dance Institute, where she and 14 other dance teachers teach 600 students. Being the sole owner, Kirstie is responsible for all business aspects of her studio. This includes everything from paying bills to mopping the floors before class. As artistic director, she determines "the artistic vision of the studio," which involves shaping and directing the focus of her studio, planning the curriculum for each class, and choreographing studio and local performances. Kirstie also includes "inspiring young girls to go after their dreams" as one of her responsibilities.

A Day on the Job

Weekends and mornings, Kirstie creates lesson plans for herself and other dance teachers and confirms teacher schedules for the week. "I teach 15 classes a week." • Around 11:30 each weekday, Kirstie heads to the studio for the "non-glorious" facets of running her business—returns phone calls, pays bills, mops, vacuums, and takes care of the studio. • Starts teaching around 4:00 p.m. and teaches for five hours straight. Her schedule usually starts with younger dancers and progresses to teen and adult classes. • Develops studio productions, which she writes, directs, and choreographs. • Choreographs for community performances.

Job Likes

Kirstie never tires of being in the classroom. She enjoys teaching, watching her dancers master a skill, and "passing on the love" of dance. "I feel like I am one of the luckiest people in the world, because I actually wake up and enjoy what I do." • "I love to dance, obviously." • "It really keeps me young and active."

Job Challenges

"There's not much I dislike about the job." The business aspect can be time-consuming and stressful, but Kirstie says, "When you go into business for yourself, you make a choice. You have to run the show. You can never give up."

Steps to Current Job

- North Carolina School of the Arts in Winston-Salem; Bachelor of Fine Arts in Contemporary Dance.
- Jumped on a Greyhound bus and headed to New York City.
- *Swing* in the European tour of *West Side Story* for two years.
- National tour of *Cats,* Victoria for two and a half years.
- Swing in the national tour of *West Side Story* for two years.
- Assistant director for the national tour of *West Side Story* for approximately two and a half years.
- Partnered in a dance studio for three years.
- Founded the North Carolina Dance Institute, where she is the owner, artistic director, and dance teacher.

Advice

Kirstie starts by saying, "a college degree is a must." She also suggests finding a mentor who will allow you to teach or to assist in teaching dance classes. You can either work for free or for pay; either way, you will gain important "hands-on" experience. Working under a mentor is important because, Kirstie says, "you have to be around kids in order to understand how to teach them." She highly recommends the teacher's training program at the National Dance Institute in New York City. She found the program to be "a crash course on how to teach kids dance in a positive manner."

"Stay focused on your goals. If you have a dream and you have a vision, go after it." Kirstie tells her students "Your friends are not going to walk through the Broadway stage door with you, so you cannot think like your friends think. You have to be your own individual person. It's your life and you only get one chance."

Helpful Personality Traits

Positive energy, never tiring, motivator, energetic, and takes care of her body.

Hobbies & Interests

Reading and outdoor activities such as hiking and rock climbing.

A *swing* is a performer who covers multiple roles in a show depending on where he or she is needed.

For more information about Kirstie's studio, see www.ncdanceinstitute.com.

"It is never too late to be what you might have been."

—George Eliot, a.k.a. Mary Ann Evans, author of *Middlemarch*

Kristi Creamer

Office Manager for a Multimedia Production Company

{ *"The biggest thing I like about it is that it's a creative environment."* }

Office manager Kristi Creamer gets a little help from her co-worker, Cake.

Job Description

Kristi oversees all of the day-to-day operations (billing, payroll, human resources, and benefits management) at the company for which she works.

A Day on the Job

Feeds the office cat. • Sorts through e-mail and responds to the most urgent ones. • Checks all bills that come in to determine which project each corresponds with. Kristi then submits them to the producers accordingly. Once the producers approve them, Kristi enters them into the company's accounting program. • Monitors employees' credit-card usage and enters receipts into the accounting program. • Oversees projects to make sure that clients are happy and that everything is on schedule and within budget. • Manages employee incentive programs, such as employee events. "We have quarterly group outings, like bowling, paintball, and baseball." Kristi also manages her company's profit-sharing and employee-recognition plans. • Updates employee manuals. • Updates employees files. • Manages payroll.

Job Likes

"The cat." • "I've seen the company grow from a small company to a bigger company." • "The biggest thing I like about it [my job] is that it's a creative environment." • Kristi edits personal videos (weddings, family events, and so on) on the side. "I'm able to use the equipment [at work] and get feedback from the people I work with."

Job Challenges

"The opportunity to move up can sometimes be limited when working for a smaller company."

Steps to Current Job

- Furman University, Greenville, South Carolina; Bachelor of Arts in Communications.
- Production assistant at a television station for four months.
- Part-time retail and temp work for four months.
- Telecommunications fraud analyst for seven months.
- Telecommunications customer service representative for one year.
- Office manager for a multimedia production company.

Advice

Kristi's route to her job isn't traditional because she has a communications degree and didn't have business experience prior to her job as office manager. In fact, many office managers have previously worked in other areas of business (such as payroll, human resources, and accounting). She also thinks that an accounting background can be helpful.

"Don't be concerned with what other people think. This is hard because I still to this day do this. You need to do what you need to do. You need to make yourself happy. Be courteous to others, and treat people the way you want to be treated; but you definitely have to look out for yourself." Kristi also thinks that it's important to experience everything you can while you're young. "Don't let fear keep you from doing something you want to do."

Helpful Personality Traits

Organized, detail oriented, diplomatic, sense of accountability, and able to delegate.

Hobbies & Interests

Basketball, editing videos, cooking, entertaining, hanging out with friends, home-improvement projects, gardening, boating, and spending time with her nephew.

Kristie Weisner Thompson

Editor for the **North Carolina Medical Journal**
and Assistant Vice President for the **North Carolina Institute**
of Medicine

{ *"It's inspiring to be exposed to people who are really passionate about what they do and also making a difference in North Carolina."* }

Job Description

As editor of the *North Carolina Medical Journal*, Kristie manages the tasks required to publish the journal six times a year. In her position as assistant vice president for the North Carolina Institute of Medicine, Kristie helps coordinate health-policy task forces. Each year, the North Carolina Institute of Medicine assembles volunteer task forces to discuss state health-care problems. Through meetings, it tries to find solutions to the problems.*

A Day on the Job

Editor of the Medical Journal

Checks e-mails for any "fires" and returns phone calls, usually to answer authors' and advertisers' questions. • Solicits, reads, and edits journal articles. "I usually have to do my reading at home." • Communicates with an advertising sales staff about schedules and advertising artwork. • Tracks advertising. For example, "I follow up and see if advertisers are going to run their classified ads again. I need to make phone calls to find out." • Works with a graphic designer on the journal layout and design. "Designing the cover is the most fun." • Coordinates the printing of each journal. "We print 25,000 copies of each issue." • Updates and maintains the Web site.

Assistant Vice President for the North Carolina Institute of Medicine

Assists in determining a yearly study topic and recommends members for the volunteer task force. "We get funding either from the state or from a private *philanthropy*." • Organizes and attends task force meetings, where she is also responsible for keeping a summary of the meeting. "We have at least one task force meeting a month, and in between those, we have smaller planning meetings. The task force meetings last all day long." • Researches information needed for the

*The North Carolina Institute of Medicine task force members are experts in the area of work that is discussed at the meetings. For more information, see www.nciom.org.

task force meetings. "Along the way, we are doing background research to find out what other states have done with similar problems." • Gathers the recommendations made by the volunteers. At the end of the year, she prepares and sends a report with the suggested recommendations to the state legislature, the North Carolina Department of Health and Human Services, philanthropic organizations, professional associations, and so on. • Updates and maintains Web site. • Writes press releases and plans press conferences.

Job Likes

"It's inspiring to be exposed to people who are really passionate about what they do and also making a difference in North Carolina. All of the folks that are on our task forces are volunteers. They don't get paid to be a part of these meetings. They share their expertise and time because they want to improve health care for people in North Carolina." • "I get to learn about a new subject every year." • "I work with great people." • Kristie likes her independent working environment. "I'm trusted to do my work. Nobody is saying, 'Have you done this? Today you're going to work on this.' I sort of set my own schedule, but have to be flexible enough to shift gears if somebody else wants something or if something comes up."

Job Challenges

"It's a lot of administrative work. I jokingly tell people I sit in front of a computer and talk on the phone all day." • "We're in a very political environment… and so we are extremely accommodating," and with Kristie's small staff, it can be challenging to please everyone.

Steps to Current Job
- University of North Carolina at Chapel Hill; Bachelor of Arts in Journalism with a concentration in Advertising.
- Editorial assistant for the computer department at UNC at Chapel Hill. Interned with an ad agency as a copywriter and also worked as a freelance copywriter.
- University of North Carolina at Chapel Hill, Master of Science in Exercise Physiology.
- Project director for research study on strokes at UNC at Chapel Hill's School of Public Health.
- Managing editor for the *North Carolina Medical Journal* and Assistant Vice President of the North Carolina Institute of Medicine.

Advice

Kristie says to ask your parents or another adult to help you find someone in hospital administration, and intern for that person. She adds, "do something besides being a lifeguard every summer. If you want to be a lifeguard one summer, then that's fine, but if you really want to figure out what you want to do, maybe be a lifeguard certain days of the week, and then spend some time in a real work environment the other days of the week. I never had a real job until after college."

"Don't discount science, and don't be afraid of it." Kristie feels that more career options would have been open to her had she applied herself in math, science, or a foreign language while in college. "Not that I had to major in them [math, science, or language], but it would have been smarter to take biology than astronomy."

Helpful Personality Traits
Organized, flexible, detail oriented, personable, journalism background is useful, team player, and resourceful.

Hobbies & Interests
Soccer, exercising, taking care of her cats, and working on her house.

The *North Carolina Medical Journal* is a bimonthly journal that covers issues dealing with the health and health care of North Carolinians. "It is a journal of health policy analysis and debate." See www.ncmedicaljournal.com for more information.

Philanthropy is the giving of funds or aid to humanitarian or artistic causes by a group or individual.

DON'T PLAY WITH BOYS

We're not suggesting that you not have relationships with guys, but this is a time in your life where your focus should be you. It's okay not to be in a steady relationship. So many women fall into the trap of falling head over heels for a man and giving up everything to be with him. If eventually you want to meet your soulmate, the things you do now will lead you to him. Being independent and having a career that you love will turn you into the kind of woman that your ultimate dream guy wants to meet.

Kristin Wolverton

High School Spanish Teacher

{ *"I love my job in July."* }

Job Description
Kristin teaches students how to communicate on a very general level in Spanish. She has many techniques, but one of her favorites is taking interested students to a Spanish-speaking country to practice conversation.

A Day on the Job
Kristin starts each morning with an hour-and-a-half planning period. Here she does the following activities: Maps out a two-week schedule for testing and class activities. "If there's something that I didn't get to do the day before that I was supposed to do, I'll revise it." • Plans tests. • Grades tests. "A lot of my time right now is spent just grading tests." • Fills out surveys to evaluate her work environment—"how safe we feel at school, how we feel the administration supports us, if we have access to all the materials we need to be effective (computers, supplies, textbooks, and so on), and whether we feel the school has a professional environment." • Plans events for students.

She then teaches three 90-minute classes, where she does the following: Assigns a warm-up activity to students, "… to get them calmed down and into the mode of Spanish." • Goes over the previous night's homework. "They'll [the students] have a chance to ask questions." • Structures the class based on whether students have grasped the previous day's lesson and homework. "Normally, I like to split it up—doing something that continues what we've learned before and then learning something new." • Introduces new information to students. • Facilitates activities that students work on in classes. "Because it is a 90-minute period, I like to vary the activities a lot. We do a little bit of writing. We do a lot of work in groups or pairs, where they can speak to each other. They do some listening activities… listen to a CD or tape and answer some questions." • Administers quizzes or tests.

Job Likes

Kristin's school is not year-round, so she has summers off. "I love my job in July." • "I like the contact with the kids." • The county where Kristin works has an established curriculum of what needs to be taught for each level of Spanish, and she says, "I like that I have a lot of freedom to do what I want to do as long as I teach the curriculum." • "I like that I'm moving around all the time. I'm not sitting at a desk all day long. I don't have someone breathing down my neck to see what I'm doing and how I'm doing." • Kristin also likes that her job allows her to introduce students to new cultures and countries. Every other year, Kristin takes her classes to a Spanish-speaking country.

Job Challenges

"Having a group of 30 students who have different learning styles... it's really hard for me to give each student individual time." • All of the teachers at Kristin's school are required to serve on a committee within the school, and Kristin says, "Sometimes it's hard to do all that and balance it with your other teaching that you have to do." • "It's hard to get done within our school hours (7:00 a.m. to 3:00 p.m.) everything that I need to get done and really be on top of things. So, normally I stay more than eight hours a day." • "I always dislike it when I have a student who acts out or is hard to manage."

Steps to Current Job

- Furman University, Greenville, South Carolina; Bachelor of Arts in Spanish.
- Lived in Spain for a semester while in school.
- Returned to Furman University to get her teaching certificate.
- Student Spanish teacher for four months.
- High school Spanish teacher for six years.
- Spanish translator for corporation for one year.
- High school Spanish teacher.

Advice

Kristin highly recommends that you go ahead and get your teaching certification before you graduate from college if you're interested in teaching Spanish. "I would also strongly suggest getting your master's degree immediately after college because I don't have my master's degree. People do it [work toward a master's degree] all the time, but I don't know how you work full time and do it." Kristin also thinks that living in a place where Spanish is the native language is a good idea. "Even if you do know the language, it's a great idea to be immersed in that culture before you try and teach it."

"You can always change your career or what you're doing. It's never too late." When it comes to day-to-day living, Kristin says, "not to worry about the little things, not to worry about things you can't control."

Helpful Personality Traits
Patient, organized, flexible, like kids, willing to try new things, and able to take and give constructive criticism.

Hobbies & Interests
Travel, reading historical fiction, beading, gardening, and fixing up her house.

Laura Bromhal

Realtor®

{ *"When you work yourself to death to get to where I am now, the business comes to me, but I am the engine that drives the business."* }

Job Description
Laura not only helps people find homes for purchase, but she also helps people sell their homes by listing them in the *Multiple Listing Service* (MLS) and following an extensive and detailed marketing plan, modified and personalized for each listing.

A Day on the Job
Laura explains that her day on the job might be a little different from someone just starting out in real estate because she has worked to achieve a level where she isn't necessarily cold calling prospective customers or out listing homes individually. She has a team that helps her do those things. Laura is so well known and respected in her community that people approach her when they are thinking about selling or buying a home. She says, "when you work yourself to death to get to where I am now, the business comes to me, but I am the engine that drives the business."

Gets up at 5:30 a.m. and prepares for her daily morning walk. • Goes on a power walk through her neighborhood. Laura sees this as self-marketing. "I walk my territory. I know every dog. I know every person, and they know I'm out there. I am famous for my walking the neighborhood. I can be walking, and someone will stop me and say, 'Laura, would you come look at my house?' or 'I've got a lead for you.'" • Attends yoga and Pilates classes. Again, Laura is constantly marketing her business by being visible in her community. • Takes constant phone calls from prospective sellers, buyers, and team members. • Hands out leads (prospective listings) to the Realtors on her team. • Attends meetings with her team to determine the status of homes listed, deal with problems, and so on. • Networks with other Realtors—for example, Laura might go to an *open house* of another Realtor because it could be a good fit for one of her customers. • Meets with real estate developers. "I've got a couple of new subdivisions that I'm dealing with, so I met with one of my developers."

Job Likes
When asked what she likes about her job, Laura says, "Everything. I love people. I love houses. I love being outside. I just have fun all day."

Job Challenges
"I'm always in competition with people for listings. To this day, a $100,000 condo—I want it. It's not the money involved. I do it because I like it." • Because of the competition involved, Laura says that other Realtors can sometimes be resentful of her success.

Steps to Current Job
- Meredith College, Raleigh, North Carolina; Bachelor of Science in Home Economics.
- Worked for her county's social services department as a secretary and as an eligibility counselor for two years.
- Became a stay-at-home mother.
- Took a real-estate certification class and passed her state's licensing exam.
- Realtor and real estate business owner. Laura has a team of eight people working for her, under York Simpson Underwood Realty.

Advice
Laura says that if you're interested in real estate, find a Realtor to shadow. She cautions that you might have to meet several to find one with a personality similar to your own. "You've gotta find somebody that's like you." In the beginning, be prepared to work a lot of hours. Laura remembers, "Every Sunday, I stood out at open houses. I met everybody… I did *phone duty*. I sat on that phone Thanksgiving, Christmas, Halloween. I sat there all day and all night. I worked 16 hours a day, seven days a week. I did that up until the last couple of years because I've got all my help. You can't keep that up or you'll burn yourself out."

Laura thinks it's important to work while you're in high school and college because you will gain all kinds of experiences, and you'll have a better idea of what you want to do with yourself. "If I had the opportunity to go and work in a real estate office, just part time, can you imagine how successful I could have been? But, heck, I didn't know what I wanted to do because I had never done anything."

Helpful Personality Traits
Approachable, motivated, and people pleaser.

Hobbies & Interests
"I'm addicted to exercise"—walking, yoga, Pilates; and socializing with friends.

> The *Multiple Listing Service* is a computer database where Realtors from all over the country put all the details about houses that they are trying to sell. Agents who work with people looking for a home to buy can search these listings online and find homes that match their clients' specifications.
>
> In real estate, an *open house* is a tool Realtors use to show a house to as many prospective buyers as possible. No appointment is necessary because the home is open for a set number of hours. People can drop in and look at their leisure.
>
> A Realtor on *phone duty* takes calls from individuals without a Realtor who might be interested in particular listings or interested in listing their own homes with the Realtor's company.

Lea Daughtridge

Director, Human Resources (HR)

{ *"Unless you really know everything involved with HR, you think it's just payroll and benefits."* }

Job Description
Lea is responsible for "all things human" at the advertising agency where she works. She oversees recruiting, training, employee relations, staffing strategies, benefits, and compensation.

A Day on the Job
Recruits for open positions in the agency. "I read a lot of resumes, interview potential candidates, offer jobs to amazing people, consult with hiring managers to determine exactly the right person for an open position, and then present candidates they might be interested in, as well as talk with outside recruiters." • Handles questions and concerns of employees. "I might have an

employee who might want to ask for a raise. I coach them on the best way to talk to their manager. At the same time, I'll have that same manager say, 'Jane just asked for a raise. What do I say?' I say, 'Here's the situation. Look at both sides.'"
• Supervises the human resources department. • Develops, writes, and introduces the agency's policies. • Manages recruitment and internship programs. • Conducts analysis and recommends the salary structure. • Researches "work-life" benefits (such as flex time, tuition reimbursement, adoption reimbursement, sabbatical programs). • Researches traditional benefit programs (health, dental, life, and disability insurance) once a year to ensure that "we are doing the right thing for our employees as well as from a financial standpoint for the agency." • Oversees a staff that handles the day-to-day operations of the agency's benefits programs. • Handles legal issues with regard to employees. • Terminates employees when necessary.

Job Likes

"No day is ever the same. Every person on this earth is different. So, everything I do is different." • "I get to learn about people, which I absolutely love." • Lea has worked in HR in the advertising industry for most of her career and says, "I don't think I could work in HR in any other industry. What I like about HR in the advertising industry is that we're really creative—out of the box, if you will." • "I get to do the good things as well as the bad things. I don't necessarily like doing the bad things, like terminating someone or dealing with a performance issue, but I know that I have a real human side about me, and that I can deliver that kind of news with feeling and empathy." • "I get to see every aspect of how we do what we do. I work with everybody." Lea thinks it's important to note that in a larger company with more than 200 employees, this is an unusual opportunity. The larger the company, the more segmented HR becomes—people's jobs become more specialized.

Job Challenges

There are a lot of people vying for creative positions in advertising, and Lea works for a leader in the industry. She says, "I'm unable to take some of the best of the best because it's hard to get in here now. I hate not being able to hire them." • "Terminating people. It's painful for me." • "I don't really like doing some of the benefits stuff… it can be boring."

Steps to Current Job
- Salem College, Winston-Salem, North Carolina; Bachelor of Arts in Communications.
- Internships at an advertising agency, a special-event planning firm, and a nonprofit art gallery.

- Special events coordinator.
- Human resources manager for distribution company
- Human resources director for an advertising agency in Boston.
- Human resources director for an advertising agency in New York City.
- Human resources director, VP for an advertising agency in Durham, North Carolina.

Advice

"HR is not a profession for someone who needs to be on the front line, who craves the limelight." That said, Lea thinks that no matter what you think you want to do, it's important to go on informational interviews—informal meetings with people to learn more about their jobs, when there is no current job opening. "Go do an informational interview with someone in a position that interests you. Ask them what they do. Ask what they like, don't like about their job, etc." With regard to her own profession, Lea reflects, "I hate the phrase 'Human Resources,' because unless you really know everything involved with HR, you think it's just payroll and benefits. It's really multidimensional. HR professionals must be knowledgeable about business strategy and serve as a partner in leading required change for the future of any corporation."

Human resources management is one place to go for information, and Lea thinks you should, "take as many classes as you can in organizational development and design."

Also, research HR in different organizations. "Successful companies, like mine, strategically leverage their HR resources; they recognize HR as a key driver of intangibles such as leadership/talent development and organizational culture."

"Get a mentor. Find somebody that you admire. It might not be somebody doing what you want to do." Lea goes on to say that you should take advantage of each and every opportunity thrown your way; and although there might be many, don't forget that "it's important for young people to be honest and live a life that they can be proud of and own."

Helpful Personality Traits

Mature, level-headed, cool under pressure, research-oriented, organized, empathetic, and firm.

Hobbies and Interests

Reading fiction, spending time with her family and dog, vacationing at the beach, volunteering in the community, decorating, and gardening.

Leonela Muñoz-Connolly

Information Technology (IT) Project Leader

{ *"Typically, you take two routes in IT. You're either the very technical expert on something or you get into the management on projects."* }

Leonela Muñoz-Connolly, IT project leader, checks the status of one of her many projects.

Job Description

Leonela assigns projects to a group of project managers that relate to the development, installation, implementation, and testing of software. She then keeps track of each project, making sure that they are progressing as they should.

A Day on the Job

Plans team members' and her own activities—"figuring out everything that needs to be done... resources we need to get it done, and assigning dates and time frames and keeping track of it as it moves forward." • Attends a lot of meetings. "A lot of what we do is coordinate activities between people and different groups and make sure that everybody knows what they're doing and when they need to do it." • Fields requests (for example, listens to problems that team members are having completing a particular project). "If there's a problem that anybody is faced with to try and get their particular piece of the project done, then it's our responsibility to figure out how to fix it. It might be that they need additional hardware. They might need additional software. They might need users' time to do testing." • Takes on projects if necessary. "There are more projects than there are of us… if the folks on my team are booked, then I take on a project."

Job Likes

"I like that I help to get things done." • She likes that she's the person who coordinates the activities between different groups that are necessary to complete a project. Leonela explains that a lot of people in the IT field don't want to attend meetings or deal with the intricacies of a project. "They're very heads down, 'I just want to do my job. I don't want to deal with other people or meetings.'" • "I like that I deal with technology. Some of what we do is analysis of business processes (how people do their jobs), so we can match that to software as well, and I love doing that."

Job Challenges

"People complaining. See, it's that double-edged sword. I'm the person that project team members call [and say], 'This is not happening; you need to help me make this happen.' It's a little frustrating to hear that all the time, but that's my opportunity to jump in and help." • "I don't know if this is something that I dislike, as much as I'd like to do more of… I'm not involved in the details, the technical aspects of the projects anymore. Typically, you take two routes in IT. You're either the very technical expert on something or you get into the management on projects."

Steps to Current Job

- University of Florida at Gainesville, Bachelor of Science in Computer Science.
- Computer programmer with a utility company for 10 years.
- Florida Atlantic University in Boca Raton, Master of Science in Mathematics.
- Teaching assistant while working on her master's.
- Actuary for one year.
- Computer programmer for two years.
- North Carolina State University, completed Master of Science coursework in Statistics.
- Teaching assistant while working on her master's.
- IT project leader.

Advice

"Get an internship to actually see what it is and maybe even do it." Leonela says that someone interested in IT might not be aware that there are two paths to take—technology or managerial. "Once you start going down the project-management road, it's not as easy to come back, and if your soul is into the technology, stay there."

"I'll tell you what I wish somebody had told me. Research and investigate all of your options. Figure out what it is that you really, really like, and stick with it. There's probably a whole slew of options related to that one thing that you like to do." Leonela half jokes, "If you cannot date until you're 25, that would be good. Okay, that's a little unrealistic, but dating seems to introduce a lot of unnecessary complications."

Helpful Personality Traits
Like to work with people, good writer and speaker, outgoing and interested in the technical aspects of IT.

Hobbies & Interests
Birding, hiking, running, fine dining, and reading biography and history books.

Li Bradshaw

Materials Chemist

{ *"The final product is the result of both the right formulation and process."* }

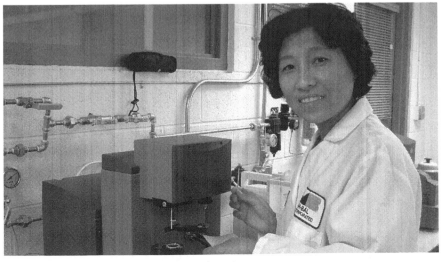
Chemist Li Bradshaw conducts a thermal analysis.

Job Description

Li works in the research and development departme:
job is to develop or improve formulations for ma
plastics products. Examples of products that a mat
industry might develop are heat-resistant parts for
and wind turbines, car parts, and tennis rackets.

A Day on the Job

Works on two to three projects a day. Usually Li has approximately five or more projects at any given time. • Studies the chemistries of related products to invent and develop new ones. • Researches and specifies materials needed for her projects. • Experiments in the laboratory to derive a chemical formula and process for the material that ultimately makes the end product. She tests physical and chemical properties of lab products to determine whether they are suitable for the application. "The final product is the result of both the right formulation and process." • Follows her project from conception through the molding and manufacturing processes. "You have to go through the whole process to make sure that the material develops… and that you can make it into a reality." • Tests the final manufactured product's chemical and physical properties to ensure that it meets all requirements. Take, for example, a plastic handle on an oven door. Is it fire- and heat-resistant? Does it retain its shape and color at high temperatures? Is it affordable?

Job Likes

"You are helping customers help other people. You see that your work is useful." • "I do have the freedom to make some decisions. There are sometimes 10 ways of making one thing. I have the freedom to make it a certain way to attain products with superior properties or processing. You have the freedom to make these decisions." • "I enjoy when projects reach fruition." • "It's very practical."

Job Challenges

When Li follows her project through the manufacturing process, the environment can be hot, dirty, and noisy. She says that proper ventilation systems, personal protection equipment, and being safety conscious are necessities. • Li finds the current job market for a materials chemist unstable.

Steps to Current Job

- Liaoning University in the Liaoning Province of China, bachelor's and master's in Chemistry.
- Chemistry instructor at a university in China.
- University of Akron in Ohio, Doctorate in Chemistry.
- *Analytical chemist* for two years.
- Materials chemist.

...gh a master's or doctorate in chemistry might not always be required ...work as a materials chemist, Li says that higher degrees help you start in a ...igher-level position and might also help you move up faster. "If you don't pursue that higher degree, then you need to spend that time at work." A materials chemist can work in a variety of industries. Some interesting examples of possible industries are cosmetics, pharmaceuticals, biotechnology, and environmental research.

"Set your career goals because with that goal in mind, you know your direction. Give your full attention to your goal."

Helpful Personality Traits
Dedicated, creative, honest, hardworking, have people skills and an aptitude for science.

Hobbies & Interests
Flower arranging and interior decorating.

> An *analytical chemist* analyzes compositions of substances.

"Luck is what happens when preparation meets opportunity."

—Seneca, Roman Philosopher

Lina Sibert

Architectural Designer

{ *"Making somebody's dream concrete... there is just so much satisfaction in that."* }

Adjunct professor and architectural designer Lina Sibert takes a quick break from drafting.

Job Description

An architect listens to someone's "dreams and desires and tries in a creative way to give them something physical that shows itself in a building. We basically build buildings from beginning to end." Lina and her husband, also an architect, own their own *design-build* architectural firm, and the majority of her clients are people either building or renovating homes.

A Day on the Job

Meets with client(s) and takes careful notes. "You listen to the words that are not spoken." She asks tons of questions about their lifestyle, such as "How do they like to live? What do they like to do?" She also asks for pictures that illustrate her clients' style preferences. Lina says, "you don't ask direct questions... a lot of people don't know what they like," so she will ask them to collect pictures of styles and features that they like in a home. • Writes a program (a description of the house)—"Basically, how many bedrooms, how big are the bedrooms, what should be next to what, what part of the house should be on the south side... how do they want to connect to the outside." Lina will get approval from her clients before proceeding any further. • Walks the site where construction will take place and thinks about her conversation with her client. "An image will start coming in my mind." • Doodles or sketches ideas. "I'll have about an inch worth of doodles." • Designs a preliminary plan and then collaborates with her co-workers about what is or isn't working. Lina will then make changes to this plan and present her design to her clients in a very informal format—"that's on trash (sketch paper), freehand." • Makes the plan more concrete and gets final approval from the client. • Develops the budget with the project manager and develops construction documents for contractors to use.

Job Likes

"I'm an introspective person… so when I'm sitting with somebody and listening to their dream, it's just so much fun. Making somebody's dream concrete… there is just so much satisfaction in that." • "I love the fact that I can sit there and stretch my mind and come up with 20 solutions and let the client choose. I just love that." • "It's always creative. It's always new. It's never boring. It's never the same—just because you're dealing with people, with different psychologies."

Job Challenges

"I wish money wasn't involved." Lina says, because often she has great ideas, but they don't always fit within her clients' budgets. • "When it gets to construction… that gets really stressful for me. I usually let other people handle that." • "I hate deadlines, but operate really well in them… because I have this nervous energy… but I'm drained after them."

Steps to Current Job

- North Carolina State University, Raleigh; Bachelor of Science in Architecture.
- Interned with an architectural firm for two years.
- University of California, Berkeley; Master of Science in Architecture.
- Architectural designer with a firm in Japan for two years.
- Architectural designer and business owner; adjunct faculty member at Meredith College, Raleigh, North Carolina.

Advice

Lina thinks that if you're interested in architecture, you have to know that you love it because "…in terms of financial reward, it's not very rewarding, so you have to do it for the sheer joy of it. Practically speaking, I would just go to somebody's [an architect's] office, and just watch. Volunteer to put away files, and ask questions." Lina also says that in life, "nothing comes easy, especially things that give you great reward. You have to work hard."

Lina grew up in Lebanon, where women are supposed to marry and not have careers. She remembers, "My dad was different. He always told us, 'You can't get married until you have a four-year degree.'" She thinks that all young women should follow this advice. Lina also says, "Know who you are, and don't worry about what people think of you. Have confidence in who you are… because then you start to worry about *what* you're doing, not about *what people think* you're doing.

Helpful Personality Traits

Love of art, mathematically inclined, excitement about solving problems, and "stick-with-it-ness."

Hobbies & Interests
Painting, sculpture, pottery, reading, and gardening.

> A *design-build* architectural firm refers to one that designs a building and then also acts as the contractor.

Lisa Carskadden

Consulting Actuary

{ *"I had no problem finding jobs whenever we moved."* }

Job Description
Lisa helps employers who offer pension (retirement) plans understand their plan's financial risks and determine how much money they need to put into them. She assists them with designing pension plans and makes sure that they are in compliance with the Internal Revenue Service and U.S. labor code requirements. Lisa also keeps her clients up-to-date with recent legislative developments and trends in the industry.

A Day on the Job
Works on several projects at a time for different clients. • Looks at U.S. Treasury regulations, Financial Accounting Standard Board statements, and U.S. Department of Labor codes and interprets them for clients. • Collects data on all the employers' plan participants (whether they are active employees or retired, and so on) and does calculations to determine the probability that people will leave for various reasons and how that will affect the value of their plan benefits. • Uses actuarial software to help her with the calculations.

Job Likes
"I like the problem solving. I obviously like math." • "I like working with people and helping my clients understand the laws and accounting rules that affect and govern their plans. It is very rewarding to be able to look through hundreds of pages of complex regulations, and then clearly explain exactly what it all means to my clients."

Job Challenges
"The bad part about being in consulting and having clients is that there can sometimes be stressful deadlines. They don't come as often as other careers, so comparatively it's not too bad." • "Hate having to deliver bad news."

Steps to Current Job
- Massachusetts Institute of Technology (MIT), Bachelor of Science in Mathematics.
- Interned as insurance actuary for an insurance company and as a financial analyst for an investment bank while in college.
- Financial analyst for an investment bank for nine months. Lisa decided that she wanted a better life balance than this job gave her. "I was working 100+ hours a week."
- Consulting actuary for a benefits consulting firm for four years.
- Consulting actuary for an accounting firm with a benefits consulting practice for two years.
- Actuarial contractor for a life insurance company for one year.
- Consulting actuary for an insurance company with a benefits consulting practice.

Advice
Lisa explains that there are two levels of actuarial exams. The first level is associateship, and the second level is fellowship. "It's almost like getting a master's degree…. When I was in college, I went ahead and signed up and took the first exam. I passed it, so when I was looking for jobs, it really helped… people were like, 'Wow, you're serious. You've already gone out there and took the time to study and take this exam and pass it.' And, they're not easy to pass." She says passing that test really gave her an edge when she was interviewing for jobs right out of college. She also thinks that her internships were a big help. Her career has been very flexible and in demand. "I had no problems finding jobs whenever we moved."

Lisa says to forget about how much different jobs pay and to "do what makes you happy. If you're not happy, no one around you is happy…. It's easy to say, but not easy to do. Look at what you enjoy doing and what you're good at. A lot of times it's the same thing."

Helpful Personality Traits
Problem solver, good at math, spreadsheet and database skills, comfortable giving presentations and speaking with clients, and good at technical writing.

Hobbies & Interests
Spending time with family, bike riding, hiking, attending theater and ballet, and planning birthday parties for her four children.

Lisa Snyder

Chief Financial Officer (CFO)

{ *"It's very challenging. I love a challenge. I get bored very easily."* }

Job Description

As CFO of a start-up insurance company, it is Lisa's job "to ensure that our financial statements are reported [both to her company's parent company and to her state's Department of Insurance] properly and to ensure the safety and soundness of the company's assets."

A Day on the Job

Ensures that all excess cash is transferred to the company's *custodial account* for investment by the investment manager. • E-mails her company's banks to let them know where to move money. • Reviews invoices. "Every single invoice that comes through here, I've got the final review on it, and it's not only reviewing to make sure that we're being billed properly, I also review to make sure that those invoices have been coded properly and that they get classified appropriately," for input into the financial system. • Reconciles receivables (money paid to her company) "to make sure that the cash coming in agrees with what is being input into the system." • Prepares accounting spreadsheets. • Calculates company losses—including known losses as well as estimating for unknown losses. • Each month Lisa and her staff have to close out the books and determine total expenses and revenue for the month (determine net income). • Prepares all financial statements for the Department of Insurance. • Ensures that the financial statement for the company is reported correctly to her parent company and to the government. • Estimates taxes. • Reviews payroll and makes sure that money is moved to the payroll account.

Job Likes

"It's very challenging. I love a challenge. I get bored very easily." • "I like math. I like solving a puzzle." • Lisa also likes that "I have the opportunity to make some decisions." Because the company that Lisa works for is a start-up company, she is determining how its financial systems will operate.

Job Challenges
"Long hours take time away from my family and my friends."

Steps to Current Job
- University of North Carolina at Asheville, Bachelor of Science in Accounting.
- Bank examiner for the State of North Carolina Banking Commission for three years.
- Internal auditor for a bank for two years.
- Commercial credit analyst at the same bank for two years.
- Received her North Carolina CPA certification.
- Financial analyst for the State of North Carolina Insurance Commission for five years.
- Senior financial analyst for the State of North Carolina Insurance Commission for three years.
- Chief financial officer.

Advice
Lisa says, "get your CPA early in the game. Be willing to spend two years in public accounting, preferably with one of the large firms. It carries tremendous weight on your resume. I feel that my career probably would have advanced a lot more rapidly had I gone that route." Working on your social side won't hurt either if you want to be a CFO. "It helps to be personable because networking is a tremendous asset in this business." Lisa also thinks that it's important to "never stop learning."

"You have to be willing to make mistakes. You'll find that you tend to be harder on yourself than anybody else, and the best lessons in life that you will learn are from making mistakes." It's important to be persistent, Lisa says. "Things don't always work out the first time, and you have to be willing to keep looking, keep searching, keep digging to get to where you want things to be. Believe in yourself. It's real easy to do things that you're comfortable with. It's scary to go out there and try something that you've never done before, and you've got to be willing to try new things."

"Find a good mentor... someone who is good at communicating with you or with other people, somebody that you respect, someone who is knowledgeable." Lisa says that if you don't know someone like that, find a friend, relative, or somebody who will help you find that person. "I think that mentors are absolutely crucial."

Helpful Personality Traits
Decisive, willing to take action, and organized.

Hobbies & Interests

Hiking, camping, biking, fishing, cars, motorcycle riding, skiing, music, and reading.

A *custodial account* is one where the assets are held (or maintained) in safekeeping, instead of being physically held by the account owner.

Lori Schantz Douglass

Freelance Advertising Copywriter

{ *"I like that I can work in coffee shops."* }

Freelance copywriter Lori Schantz Douglass makes a coffee-shop courtyard her office.

Job Description

Lori writes and develops advertising campaigns that appear in media such as TV, radio, newspapers, and magazines. Depending on the assignment, she might work with an advertising agency or directly with a company. Lori sees her job as thinking of the "simplest, most powerful way to convey an idea about a product or service."

A Day on the Job

Determines weekly child care for her children based on jobs assigned. • Checks e-mail regarding new assignments and revisions on current assignments. • Researches the clients' products as well as competitive products and competitive advertising. • Concepts/brainstorms ideas with her partner (the art director). "Work, work, and work some more and pray that an idea comes." The two of them make sure the idea has "legs" and can work for a campaign. • Presents ideas to clients for approval/revisions. "There are often many levels of approvals and many rounds of revisions." • Writes copy to go with the "big idea" that she and her partner have developed. • Meets with or sends her *portfolio* (a book of her past projects) to prospective clients when she is not actively working on projects.

Job Likes

"I love coming up with ideas." • Lori enjoys the creative energy she has with her partner and says, "It's fun bouncing ideas back and forth." • "You learn a lot about a lot of different products and industries. I've worked on accounts ranging from cars to carpets to cruises to utilities to women's extra-large undergarments." • "I like the flexibility." She can dress the way she wants, and her schedule allows time to spend with her two small children. "Since I don't have to work in an office, I don't have to dress up or wear makeup. I have no one to scare but myself." • "I don't have to deal with office politics—a big plus." • "I like working with creative people—they're interesting, intelligent, and more than a little kooky." • "When you produce television commercials, you get to travel to some fabulous places." • "I can work in coffee shops. Cappuccinos make for cheap rent."

Job Challenges

"Tight deadlines. You don't always know when you're going to come up with an idea, and that can be stressful." • "There's too much commercialism in the world, and I'm contributing to it. I struggle with that." • Lori is responsible for all business decisions such as taxes, computer equipment, insurance, and supplies, and says, "…because I'm a creative person, I don't necessarily like the business end of things." • Lori works at home a lot and laments, "It can get lonely not working with people everyday." • Keeping Lori's portfolio up-to-date can be difficult because she isn't always involved in the production of her ideas, so she doesn't always have a finished product to put in her book. • "Reactions to your ideas are very subjective. People can have very different opinions about what constitutes a good idea."

Steps to Current Job
- University of North Carolina at Chapel Hill, Bachelor of Arts in Journalism.
- Advertising copywriter for six years.
- Senior advertising copywriter for six years.
- Freelance advertising copywriter.

Advice
In addition to obtaining an undergraduate degree, most copywriters attend a two-year program at a school such as The Portfolio Center or Creative Circus to work on putting their books together. Lori says, "It's almost a requirement to do that now." If you want to bypass the additional years of school, there may be agencies where you can intern (perhaps unpaid) and put together a portfolio using the creative staff as mentors.

Lori says, "Even in this day and age, there are certain issues that can be more difficult for women. For example, if you want to have children, you have to consider how your career will be altered. That's an issue that, generally speaking, many men still don't have to worry about as much. That being said, I think that you should go after your dreams, whatever they are. You can't plan all of your life at once."

Helpful Personality Traits
Avid reader, liberal arts background, flexible, thick skinned because your ideas will often be harshly judged, and able to work with many different personalities.

Hobbies & Interests
Reading, cooking, love of outdoors, and spending time with friends.

A *portfolio* (or "book") is a collection of a writer's, art director's, or artist's best work, which they use to help them get future jobs.

Lorie Ann Morgan

Patent Attorney for a Pharmaceutical Company

{ *"It's rewarding because what I do, in part, is a benefit to society. I'm involved in getting new drugs and new therapies to treat human disease on the market, and I'm very proud of that."* }

Job Description

Lorie Ann's job is to obtain *patents* to protect inventions that are made by her company and to enforce those patents through litigation if necessary. Patents are sometimes the only effective way of protecting a company's product or process and earning back the money it spent in developing the product.

A Day on the Job

Provides legal advice to people within her company about how to best accomplish their goals. "I spend a lot of time talking to people and giving them some advice on what course of action they should take." For example, if a drug has been developed and her company wants to get it to market, Lorie Ann makes sure that it has a patent and all of the legal protection necessary to keep other companies from copying it. • Works a lot with the regulatory department of her company to ensure that the drug that they are getting Federal Drug Administration (FDA) approval for is the same drug/chemical combination that Lorie Ann's team has patented. • Files lawsuits when notified by the FDA of a competing company's plan to sell a copy of one of her company's drugs. • Reads a lot of materials. "It could be any number of things. For example, I could be reading a patent application that we would like to see granted as a patent. I could be reading patents from another company. I could be reading materials for publication by individuals in the company to decide whether or not we should file patent applications before we publish. Things like that." • Writes papers to get a particular patent application to a point where the Patent and Trademark Office will give it a patent. • Provides guidance and advice to younger, less experienced patent attorneys. "I'll help them with particular problems."

Job Likes

"I like everything about it. I really enjoy the challenges that I'm faced with every day because every day is different." • "It's rewarding because what I do, in part, is a benefit to society. I'm involved in getting new drugs and new therapies to treat human disease on the market, and I'm very proud of that." • "I love to write patent applications… and I like to enforce those patents to make sure that my company gets all of the rights that they're entitled to." • "I like the people that I work with."

Job Challenges

"I'm not one that loves to travel, and this job necessitates a fair amount of travel; but I've gotten so good at travel that it doesn't bother me anymore."

Steps to Current Job

- University of North Carolina at Wilmington, Bachelor of Arts in Chemistry and Bachelor of Arts in Political Science.
- University of North Carolina at Chapel Hill Law School, Juris Doctorate.
- Law clerk (intern) for two and a half years while in law school.
- Associate for law firm where she clerked for five years.
- Associate for a different firm for 14 months.
- Senior patent counsel, director of pharmaceutical patents.

Advice

To practice patent law, you have to have an undergraduate degree in some field of science, so Lorie Ann suggests, "identify the area of science that you like, and seek out a patent attorney that practices in that area. All of the patent attorneys I know, and certainly myself, are so delighted when someone in college or in law school, or even high school, calls me up and says, 'could you come down here and talk to me, or this group of people about what it is you do.'" She says to ask them hard questions: What is it that they like? What is it that they don't like? What's not fun? What do they do all day?

"I think that one of the biggest distractions that young women face as they're trying to move forward in their career and their education is, to be frank, the presence of men. Your life will be so much richer, and you'll be so much happier, if you feel the confidence that comes from knowing that you can take care of yourself. Marriage, children, all of that will come. First it's so important to understand yourself, to know who you are, and to feel comfortable in your own independence. Once you do that, everything in your life will be so much easier."

Lorie Ann thinks that young women should take at least a year off between their education and starting their careers. "If I had to do it over again, I would temper my ambition, and take that year to get life experience. I've been practicing law for 11 years, and I'm looking at another 35 years of practicing law, and I'm never going to have the opportunity to take a year and explore other cultures. The only opportunity you have is when you're in that growing process… in school."

Helpful Personality Traits
Desire to be meticulous, focused, and a love of puzzles.

Hobbies & Interests
Reading anything and everything—classics, new comedies, drama, nonfiction, and so on; cooking; riding her motorcycle; running; downhill and cross-country skiing; sewing; quilting; playing with her dogs; watching football; gardening; and tackling home-improvement projects.

A *patent* is a monopoly granted by a country that allows its owner to prevent others from using an invention. For more information on patents, see the United States Patent and Trademark Office Web site at www.uspto.gov.

Louanne DiBella

Jewelry and Product Designer and Product Development Specialist

{ *"I've never had a job that didn't involve a lot of creativity."* }

Job Description
Louanne designs jewelry and decorative home products. Many of her designs are for popular lines seen in major department stores. Home products include items such as picture frames, candles, clocks, and purse accessories. As a product development specialist, Louanne helps people produce an idea or product. "If someone has an idea or an item that they've designed or invented, but they don't know how to develop it with the manufacturer, I can help them with that."

A Day on the Job
Jewelry and Product Design
Meets or speaks with her client to discuss the product he or she needs designed. "I go up [to New York City] probably every two to three months for either a runway show or a meeting." • Organizes her schedule to meet deadlines. "I try to figure out how much time it's going to take me per day in order to get me to that

deadline." • Researches to find inspiration for her designs. This might include attending fashion shows, exploring bookstores, visiting libraries, or searching the Internet. • Sketches product ideas. "I do it all by hand." • After receiving approval of sketches from her client, she draws or paints her designs using gouache (watercolor) and acrylic paints. • Sends final designs to her client. "I'm providing people with designs, and then they take it and have it made."

Product Development
Client presents her with an idea or product he or she wants manufactured. • Louanne uses contacts all over the world to help design, sculpt, mold, and produce the product. The majority of the manufacturers she uses are in China, Korea, and Thailand.

Job Likes

Because Louanne is a freelance artist, she has the flexibility to decide her own schedule. "I can have as much or as little work as I want." This freedom is also valuable while raising her young child. • Louanne enjoys that her job takes her to New York City every couple of months. "I'm living in the country, but every now and then I get to fly up and get that dose of city." • "I've never had job that didn't involve a lot of creativity."

Job Challenges
"Right now, I can't think of one thing."

Steps to Current Job
- Attended high school at the North Carolina School for the Arts in Winston-Salem; majored in Visual Arts.
- The University of the Arts in Philadelphia, Pennsylvania; Bachelor of Fine Arts in Jewelry and Metalsmithing.
- Worked as jewelry designer for 11 years for various companies starting as an assistant and working her way up to senior designer.
- Decorative home-product designer for two years.
- Freelance jewelry and product designer and product development specialist.

Advice
"The art background is essential... preferably a four-year degree; a two-year degree could probably get you in if you're very talented." Louanne also says that working for many different companies benefited her because she learned more about her craft and the business, and she made many contacts, which helps her working as a freelance artist. "I learned the business of each company. I also met a lot of buyers for all the big stores. So I have a huge Rolodex of names and numbers, and that is the secret to a lot of success—who you know."

"Really explore job potential." Louanne says that there are many types of jobs out there that are creative and interesting, but that you have to think outside of the box. "I think the best thing to do is to reach and call people and talk to people, and don't be afraid to cold-call people. That's how I got into the business— just cold-calling people out of the newspapers. Knock on as many doors as you can, and somebody will let you in eventually."

Helpful Personality Traits
Artistic, creative, aggressive (Louanne finds this helpful in a corporate atmosphere), assertive, and a good public speaker.

Hobbies & Interests
Painting, drawing, gardening, cooking, entertaining, Pilates, and family.

FRIENDSHIPS MADE AT WORK

So many of the women we talked with said that they really enjoy their co-workers and think of them as friends. It might seem like that's something you have no control over, but when you're doing something that you love, the odds are that your co-workers feel the same way about their jobs. And, you will probably have a lot more in common than just work. Work relationships are something to look forward to when establishing your career.

Lynda Heymen

Clinical Psychologist

{ *"When I'm old and crossing over, hopefully I'll have a lot of satisfaction and feel that I made a difference."* }

Job Description
Lynda talks with individual patients or couples about what mental-health challenges they face and changes they want to make, and what strategies they can use to go about making those changes.

A Day on the Job

Reviews charts. "I start my day by reviewing the charts of the patients I'm going to see that day." • Sees patients on the hour with a break for lunch (generally from about 10:00 a.m. until 7:00 p.m.). • Records progress notes. "In my charts I have written what we accomplished and where we want to go."

Job Likes

Lynda's job allows her to be a "healer," and that gives her life meaning. "I can't begin to explain the joy that you have when you see somebody building up the confidence to actually take the risks necessary to be successful." • "When I'm old and crossing over, hopefully I'll have a lot of satisfaction and feel that I made a difference." • "It gives me a way to be creative. No two people are alike. No two sets of problems are alike. No two relationships are alike." Lynda says that she is constantly drawing from her education and from her professional and personal experiences to help people get past the blocks they have.

Job Challenges

Because psychotherapy involves weekly visits to a psychologist, Lynda has to be flexible with her patients' work schedules, and she doesn't necessarily like working at night. "I was told long ago that there would be no way to avoid it in private practice." • Liability is another part of the job that causes her stress. "We can't be responsible for other people. They have to be responsible for themselves. If someone is determined to commit suicide, they probably will. I'm always monitoring those risk situations carefully and try not to miss a clue... that piece of it, I think, the average therapist would say is the toughest." • "There are some people that never get to the place of being accountable in life. They never really take responsibility for themselves, and they don't do well in therapy. It's always very sad to watch that and to have to end the relationship."

Steps to Current Job
- University of Tennessee at Knoxville, Bachelor of Science in Wildlife and Fisheries Science.
- University of Tennessee at Knoxville, Master of Science in Wildlife and Fisheries Science.
- *Strip-mine reclamation* program developer for the State of Alabama for one year.
- Nova Southeastern University, Fort Lauderdale, Florida; Master of Science and doctoral degree in Clinical Psychology.
- *Biofeedback* therapist for seven years.
- Private-practice psychotherapist for nearly 20 years.

Advice

Lynda says to ask yourself why you're interested in psychology. If you're always "the therapist" in your relationships, that's not a good reason to go into this field, and "usually comes from some dysfunction in the family. You need to understand that, and work through that, and then ask yourself, 'Is this really something I want to do?'" Once you decide that clinical psychology is for you, Lynda thinks that you should shadow several different types of psychologists, such as school psychologists and organizational psychologists. You won't be able to go into private sessions with a clinical psychologist, but interviewing a private-practice psychologist can give you a lot of insight into the field. Volunteering is also a great way to get a glimpse of the field. Lynda did intake screenings at a mental health clinic, and that allowed her to be on the inside and see the issues that psychologists deal with on a day-to-day basis.

"When you're a child, be a child. Don't try to grow up too fast… because it's a very special time, and you'll never get it back. You're supposed to be doing important things during that period. You're supposed to be forming an identity."

Helpful Personality Traits

Emotionally sensitive, empathic, strong values, and willing to work on yourself (getting your own therapy).

Hobbies & Interests

Dance (Lynda teaches Nia [neuromuscular integrative action] three times a week), canoeing, hiking, camping, gardening, reading, and discussing spiritual philosophies and approaches to life.

> **Biofeedback** is a technique that helps people voluntarily regulate physiological functions, such as heart rate or muscle tension, to promote relaxation.
>
> **Strip-mine reclamation** is restoring mine sites to prevent erosion and chemical runoff.

Macon Riddle

Antiques-Shopping Consultant and Owner of Let's Go Antiquing

{ *"Make your work your play… I don't feel like I'm really working."* }

Antique-shopping consultant and owner of Let's Go Antiquing, Macon Riddle, finds treasure for her clients.

Job Description

Macon "dreamed up" this business while she was working in an antiques store. New Orleans' French and Spanish history make it a prime tourist destination and a wonderful place to find European antiques. Macon takes tourists, who are unfamiliar with New Orleans' antiques market, to various dealers and answers any questions that they have. She helps clients find a specific item or gives them an overview of the world of antiques in New Orleans. Macon puts no pressure on her clients to buy and always helps them get the best price. She says, "they ultimately make the decision."

A Day on the Job

Plans her day based on the types of antiques her clients want to purchase. • Picks up clients. "I pick up the people at the hotel... and I head in the direction that I think will interest them." • Answers any antiques questions that clients might have. • Gauges her clients' needs and enthusiasm. "As the shopping goes along, I will probably alter or add or subtract some of the things that I thought might appeal to them [clients]. People will also change their mind about what they're looking for."

Job Likes

"I love meeting people." • "I love the learning. When you're dealing with antiques, you're always learning." • "I like helping people find what they're looking for. I like the satisfaction. I like giving people an overview. I get energized helping people."

Job Challenges
"I think I was surprised at how hard I was going to have to work at marketing... you have to sell yourself, and that takes some work."

Steps to Current Job
- Mary Baldwin College, Stanton, Virginia; studied history and religion for three years.
- George Washington University, Washington, D.C.; Bachelor of Arts in History and Religion.
- History and English teacher for three years.
- Full-time mother to three for 27 years. She was a substitute teacher throughout this time.
- Part-time work for an antiques dealer for 13 years. "I had never been exposed to French furniture. So much to learn, and I just loved it."
- Owner of Let's Go Antiquing.

Advice
Macon says that to do what she does, you need to live in a large city that supports a lot of antiques. "Over the years, I've talked to people in Atlanta and Charleston... it's not quite enough quantity and diversity." Don't forget to "make your work your play. I don't feel like I'm really working."

Macon asks, "Would it sound corny to say, 'follow your dreams?' If you're determined, and you really want to do something, there is a way."

Helpful Personality Traits
People person, extrovert, organized, good physical shape, enthusiastic, and skilled at getting along with all different types of people.

Hobbies & Interests
Antiquing, gardening, travel, and my house.

To learn more about Macon's business, see www.neworleansantiquing.com.

Note: Macon's home and business were spared by 2005's Hurricane Katrina, but her business will suffer until tourists return to New Orleans. "My Let's Go Antiquing will be slow for a while, but I am confident it will come back as the city does. New Orleans has survived floods, yellow fever, epidemics, wars, and depression. The shops in the French Quarter are fine, as are the ones on Magazine Street. We just need visitors."

Margaret Gamble

Elementary School Media Specialist (a.k.a. Librarian)

{ *"One of the most important things that I try and get across is to teach students how to learn."* }

Job Description
Margaret oversees all of the functions of her school's library. In the process, she serves all of the media needs of the students and teachers.

A Day on the Job
Gets the library up and running—"That means powering up the library server computer... all the doors open and ready for business." • Margaret teaches library classes in 30- or 45-minute blocks. "Just like there's a science curriculum, math curriculum, I have a curriculum that I have to teach as well. You start out with print literacy. What is the front of a book? What do you call it? What's the title page? What is an author? What is an illustration? You start teaching call numbers and shelving processes." Margaret also teaches the exploration of literature: plot, character development, and character analysis. • Helps students and teachers locate any materials they might need. • Fulfills administrative duties for the library, such as "a lot of technology repair kind of stuff, budget items that come up, placing purchase orders."

Job Likes
"I like the kids." • "I like sharing the stories and educating them as to what good literature is." • Margaret gets a lot of satisfaction out of teaching students how to track down information. "One of the most important things that I try and get across is to teach students how to learn... to know how to find answers to questions that they come up with, not necessarily because it's on a test or a teacher wants them to know." • Margaret ended our interview by saying, "I hope that I conveyed how much I love this job and how much I think other women would love this job."

Job Challenges

"I feel like I'm doing two jobs." In addition to the curriculum that Margaret has to teach and the library services that she provides, she is also responsible for facilitating technology issues in the library and classrooms.

Steps to Current Job

- University of West Florida, Pensacola, Bachelor of Arts, Legal Administration.
- Volunteered for criminal defense and public defender's office while in college.
- Paralegal for civil defense law firm for a year and a half.
- Stay-at-home mom for five years and worked toward her teaching certification.
- Elementary substitute teacher for six months.
- Title I assistant at school, where she substituted for four years.
- East Carolina University, Greenville, North Carolina; Master of Library Science (MLS).
- Elementary school media specialist.

Advice

Although most young women do not have a problem rapidly adapting to technology, Margaret says it's important to have these skills because they can definitely be incorporated into the teaching of media and literature. As a counterbalance to that, she thinks, "you have to want to have fun. To work with children and hold 25 kids' attention for 30 minutes, you have to be pretty outgoing and dramatic and have a bit of ham bone in you." Margaret wants people to know that it's a misconception that librarians are very serious and like things quiet. With regard to educational requirements, she says most states require certification to be a school media specialist, and to get it you have to have the MLS degree.

"I have a 13-year-old, and what I really try and preach to her is 'Pay less attention to the people around you and more attention to the person you're going to be.'" Experiencing the world can help you do this. "If you have a bigger, wider appreciation of a multitude of cultures and circumstances and beliefs, it helps define who you are; but it also gives you a better perspective where we [Americans] are in the world." Margaret's last bit of advice, "Ignore the boys."

Helpful Personality Traits

Inquisitive, enjoy tracking down answers, and entertaining.

Hobbies & Interests

Reading, gardening, travel to the beach, fixing things up, and antiquing.

Maria Kelly-Doggett

Chemical Engineer

{ *"There are opportunities for chemical engineers in a wide variety of locations."* }

Job Description

Working as a chemical engineer for a pharmaceutical company, Maria's job is to develop and improve production processes. According to the American Institute of Chemical Engineers, chemical engineers use "their knowledge of mathematics and science—particularly chemistry—to overcome technical problems safely and economically." For Maria, development includes choosing the right manufacturing equipment and finding the right operating conditions for the process. Operating conditions refer to temperature, pressure, pH, and so on. She might also evaluate existing processes to improve product quality, reduce production cost, and minimize environmental impact.

A Day on the Job

Checks on the production process by visiting or calling the production area or checking computer data. If there is a problem, it must be dealt with immediately • Works on current projects such as developing improvements in the production process or working to install new equipment. Project duties can range from working in the laboratory fine-tuning a process to talking on the phone with an equipment vendor about equipment designs. • Writes reports that summarize projects, usually for internal purposes. • Supervises technical specialists. • Attends company meetings to talk about a specific project.

Job Likes

"I like the fact that it is mentally challenging. It's not the same thing everyday." • "It's a job that if I need to I am able to support my family." • "The type of job that I had, it allowed me to interface with people in varying levels of the organization." • "There are opportunities for chemical engineers in a wide variety of locations."

Job Challenges

"Some of the production environments are very noisy; you get exposed to potentially hazardous chemicals and to things that can explode or catch fire." • "I'm not very good at office politics… that's not my personality."

Steps to Current Job

- North Carolina School of Science and Math in Durham; last two years of high school.
- North Carolina State University in Raleigh; Bachelor of Science in Chemical Engineering, minor in Spanish.
- Chemical engineer for a pharmaceutical company for six and a half years.
- Meredith College, Raleigh, North Carolina; Master of Business Administration while working for the pharmaceutical company.
- Chemical engineer for an oil refinery for two and a half years.
- Chemical engineer for a pharmaceutical company for three and a half years.
- Currently taking time off for pregnancy.

Advice

In high school, study your math and science. "That goes without saying." In college, "try to get into a co-op program." (A co-op is when you work every other semester for a company in your field of study.) Maria finds co-ops beneficial for many reasons. They give you hands-on experience, allow you to figure out whether the career is right for you, help you make contacts in your field, and help pay for school. Maria also points out that in a co-op, "you get to figure out what you do and don't like and it helps you to be more selective when you go to look for a job."

Maria's corporate work experience has taught her that being assertive is important. Don't be afraid to ask for what you want. She also thinks that it's important to remember that "a career is always evolving. If you're not happy with it, try something else."

Helpful Personality Traits

Inquisitive and possess an aptitude for science and math.

Hobbies & Interests

Cooking, spending time with family, walking, and traveling.

For more information, see the Web site of the American Institute of Chemical Engineers (AIChE) at www.aiche.org.

Marie Baker

Retired Field Supervisor for Nursing Assistants for a Home-Health Agency

{ *"I enjoyed the freedom to be out traveling about, meeting different people and being in all types of environmental settings."* }

Retired nurse Marie Baker demonstrates her nursing skills to her grandson, Josh Snyder.

Job Description

Prior to retiring, Marie worked as a field supervisor to nurses' aides who worked for a home-health-care provider. She made sure that all nurses' aides followed proper procedures so that patients received the best possible care.

A Day on the Job

Coordinated nurses' aides' schedules and her schedule for evaluating them. • Observed nurses' assistants in the field, specifically looking at infection control, patient-care techniques, and safety for both the aide and the patient. "Every patient had to have a regulated number of visits by a supervisor and every nursing assistant had to be supervised [in the field] so many times over the course of a year." • Documented forms detailing these observations.

Job Likes

"I enjoyed the freedom to be out traveling about, meeting different people and being in all types of environmental settings... not having to be behind a desk all day long." • "I've always been interested in community health."

Job Challenges

"I disliked the paperwork required by the *Joint Commission on Accreditation of Heathcare Organizations (JCAHO)* and the Medicare regulations." • Marie says that when dealing with people's lives, nursing can be stressful.

Steps to Current Job

- W.A. Foote Memorial Hospital/Jackson Junior College, Jackson, Michigan; associate degree.
- Surgical nurse/intensive care nurse for one year.
- Emergency-room nurse for one year.
- Part-time pediatric nurse for four years.
- Part-time general nurse for eight years.
- Home-health nurse for one year.
- Psychiatric nurse for 12 years.
- Home-health nurse and supervisor for nine years.

Advice

Marie says, "Home-health nurses need a variety of nursing experiences." So, if you want to pursue this particular branch of nursing, experience in surgery, pediatrics, mental health, intensive care, and emergency room, as well as other types of nursing, is invaluable. "To have all of this varied background helps you with all of these individual problems that are very different from case to case and from patient to patient in the home." Marie thinks that if you're interested in nursing, you need to know yourself. "If you are a person who tends to be nervous, this profession can create a lot of anxiety."

She also believes that you should visit all of the professions that interest you and to get as much work experience as possible doing anything. "The more interactions you have with people and job experiences you have before you start actually thinking and settling on a career, the more you'll get to know yourself and get to know how you deal with people."

Hobbies & Interests

Gardening, walking, reading, travel, playing cards, and swimming.

Helpful Personality Traits

Calm, low anxiety level, direct/good communicator, and willing to be a patient advocate (stick up for the patient).

The *Joint Commission on Accreditation of Healthcare Organizations* is an independent, not-for-profit organization that evaluates more than 16,000 health-care organizations in the United States.

Mary Thorn

Senior Computer Software Quality Assurance Analyst

{ *"Very few people do what I do."* }

Job Description
Mary tests software and makes sure that it works correctly. The company where she works creates Web-based human resource software used by companies for online employment applications. Her company has more than 130 clients, each using different software features, and Mary is responsible for testing any changes and added functions.

A Day on the Job
Copies altered software from the developer (computer programmer) and moves it to her computer server to prepare it for testing. • Tests software and verifies that changes are working correctly by comparing the new version to the existing version. • Moves software to a server where the client can verify that changes are working correctly.

Job Likes
Mary loves her boss because "she lets me do what I want to do." Mary's job allows her the flexibility to focus on her passion—refereeing basketball. • "I rarely work 40 hours… as long as I get my work done, that's all that matters."

Job Challenges
"There's not much growth in the job."

Steps to Current Job
- East Carolina University, Greenville, North Carolina; Bachelor of Science in Business Administration with a concentration in Management Information Systems (MIS).
- Senior consultant with a consulting firm for 18 months.
- Quality assurance (QA) analyst for one year.
- Manager of quality assurance for two years.
- Senior quality assurance analyst.

Advice
"You definitely have to have a computer background… whether it be MIS or CIS [Computer Information Systems]." Mary also thinks that a math degree is helpful. "Interestingly enough, a lot of people who are QA people sometimes start as support people who answer the phone and deal with the software on the front end with the client. They actually find out a lot of problems that way. Their next step is QA because they've dealt with so many problems." Another avenue into software quality assurance is to work as a developer first.

"Find whatever it is that you're passionate about. I had sports. My friends had other things." Mary also says, "there are a lot of ways to make money, and if you're passionate about it, you can start at the age of 10, 15, or 20 doing those things."

Helpful Personality Traits
Attention to detail, organized, and a love of computers and software.

Hobbies & Interests
Refereeing, traveling, spending time with friends, and going to movies.

Michelle Owen

Graphic Designer

{ *"If you're designing without any particular goal, you're not visually communicating anything other than a pretty picture, and that's not what design is about."* }

Job Description

After thoroughly researching her design subject, Michelle creates a design that visually communicates a message (or messages). The majority of her work entails creating *corporate identity* and *publication design*. Michelle is self-employed and has a design studio in her house. "I laughingly say I have a corner office with a view."

A Day on the Job

Presents her portfolio to prospective clients. "You set up an initial interview to do a portfolio showing to see if your design style is something that they're looking for. Once you establish that they want to work with you, you decide what the goals are for their project." • Researches the product/service that her designs will promote. • Starts the design process using her research and the client's goals to guide her. The computer is her main design tool. She uses a variety of graphic-design software to help her develop her ideas. • Takes the preliminary design to the client for his or her approval—"to see if anything needs to be tweaked or changed." • Finishes the design and gets final approval from her client. • Sends files to the printer for production, where she oversees the job for her client as it is being printed.

Job Likes

Michelle did not want a desk job, and the research each project requires grants her a certain amount of freedom. "People don't understand that design is probably 90 percent research and 10 percent actual hands-on design. If you're designing without any particular goal, you're not visually communicating anything other than a pretty picture, and that's not what design is about." • "It's constantly changing; there's never the same project twice." She says that she is "always thinking about things in different ways because different clients have different objectives." • "If you own your own studio, you are your own boss, so you don't have to worry about somebody else telling you what to do all the time."

Job Challenges

"You really need to pick and choose your projects according to your personal morals." For example, Michelle is against the use of tobacco, so she would never take on a job that promoted the use of it.

Steps to Current Job

- Blue Ridge Community College in Hendersonville, North Carolina; general courses.

- Western Carolina University in Cullowhee, North Carolina; Bachelor of Fine Arts with a concentration in Graphic Design. "I actually dropped out at one point. I loved working more than I liked to be in school." Michelle worked in sign shops while attending school. She also took some art and design classes at the Art Institute of Atlanta while taking a break from Western Carolina University.
- Graphic designer for a publishing company for six years. Among her responsibilities were designing book covers. Michelle interned for this company while attending Western Carolina University.
- Owner of a design firm for three years.

Advice

"Learn everything about everything because it all comes into play in design." When you're creating a design, you are pulling information from many areas. Everything about your target market should be taken into consideration, such as their political views, history, culture, and so on. "It's not just about art, it's about communication." Michelle suggests minoring in a subject that supports the direction you want to take your graphic-design skills. For example, a minor in business is helpful for owning your own design firm, whereas a minor in management is beneficial if being a manager/director is your goal.

"My big thing is challenge everything, but know when to voice it and know when not to voice it. Just because you don't agree with somebody doesn't always mean that you're right or they're wrong."

Helpful Personality Traits

A good mix of introvert/extrovert, patient, able to visualize problems and solutions, multitasker, organized, able to communicate with all kinds of people, and a good listener.

Hobbies & Interests

Quilting, crocheting, board games, time with family, and card games.

Corporate identity pertains to developing or utilizing existing company logos and making sure that the company's image is consistent in its stationery, advertising, marketing, and so on.

Publication design pertains to multipage publications such as magazines, brochures, pamphlets, books, catalogs, newsletters, and so on.

Molly Rogers

Emmy®-Award-Winning Costume Designer

{ *"I absolutely adore going to a* haute couture *show in Paris."* }

Costume designer Molly Rogers soaks up the sun in the city where her dreams came true.

Job Description

Molly is a costume designer for television shows, commercials, and movies. One of her most notable claims to fame is working for the television show *Sex and the City.* For each job, she "reads, analyzes, and conceptualizes" the script and talks with the director "to determine what clothes belong on each character." Molly shops for the clothing either in showrooms or at retail stores, and then has a fitting with the actors.

A Day on the Job

Determines the clothes needed for each character. • Shops for the clothes by visiting stores, attending fashion shows, making them, or renting them. "I'm not the only one shopping. I have two assistants and then my partner that I work with." • Fits the costumes to the actors. • Helps manage the department to make sure deadlines are met—"making sure everything that needs to happen that day, happens."

Job Likes

"I did not want to punch in at 9 and punch out at 5. So the one thing I love about my job is that every single day is different. Every day is an adventure." • "I also get to work with dynamic people in many different departments such as directors, producers, writers, and hair and makeup." • "I absolutely adore going to a *haute couture* show in Paris. Those are amazing spectacles to witness. It is so exciting and the clothes are so exquisite."

Job Challenges

"There's nothing routine about it, so there can be pleasant and unpleasant surprises." • "It's stressful. A lot of the stress is about the time that you have to do things. The pace of television is kind of like a train that just keeps coming. While you're reading one script, you're shooting another one."

Steps to Current Job
- Meredith College in Raleigh, North Carolina.
- University of North Carolina at Chapel Hill, Bachelor of Arts in Psychology.
- Worked for a clothing store in London, England for two years (during the '80s punk era).
- Moved to New York City and worked for a popular clothing store, where she started styling artists for music videos.
- Became a freelance costume designer for commercials, television, and movies.

Advice

Molly believes the best training is actual work experience. She suggests doing an internship in the field by working for your local theatre wardrobe department, advertising agencies, or television stations.

"Dream big! Whatever you think is possible is truly possible. Reinforce your self-esteem by telling yourself everyday what a great person you are and how life is full of possibilities and how you want to touch all of them. As small or large a task may be, take pride and learn from everything and everyone you encounter. Taking time to have a vision of what you want from your life can give you insight and goals to reach. Having an open, nonjudgmental mind can give you opportunities that will ultimately benefit you in all aspects in your life." Molly also recommends reading and traveling because they both "open up the world" to you.

Helpful Personality Traits

A good listener, get along with all people, and honest (Molly finds this highly appreciated in her business).

Hobbies & Interests
Reading, yoga, and travel.

> A *haute couture* show is an exclusive fashion show where leading designers present one-of-a kind designs. The designs are exquisitely detailed and made by hand. Haute couture shows are attended by a select audience, including some of the most powerful and wealthiest people. "Design details from these shows are usually honed in on and made affordable for the ready-to-wear public."

"Well-behaved women seldom make history."

—Laurel Thatcher Ulrich, author, *The Midwife's Tale*

Natalie Woods

Paramedic

{ *"We can do anything from putting a Band-Aid on someone to performing CPR."* }

Paramedic Natalie Woods is still smiling after a long shift of responding to emergencies.

Job Description

Natalie works on an ambulance and serves the public by answering emergency medical calls. She is on call at her base station either 12 or 24 hours at a time, two or three days a week.

A Day on the Job

Checks out the ambulance. "You have to go through every piece of equipment and every medication... check expiration dates, check to make sure the equipment is working properly, make sure you have the necessary equipment." Natalie also checks the maintenance of the truck—fluid levels, tires, and so on. • Reports any problems that she finds in her truck check. • Fills out paperwork that tracks the use of narcotics on medical calls. • Attends to base duties when she's not on the ambulance: "taking out the trash, cleaning the floors, the bathrooms, making sure that everything is neat and tidy and where it needs to be." • Folds and packages linens for use on the ambulance. • Communicates on the radio with the dispatcher and other emergency workers. • Drives to any emergency situation to which she is called, including fire calls, where she monitors the health and well-being of the firefighters and victims. • Treats patients according to protocol set by the emergency director of the county where she works. • Writes up information about each emergency call using standardized forms. • Notifies the hospital ahead of time "to let them know what kind of situation we have going on." • Communicates patient condition and care received upon arrival at hospital.

Job Likes

"I really like being out in the public and dealing with people. What's interesting about this job is that I get to see people sometimes at their best and sometimes at their very, very worst." • "I like my co-workers."

Job Challenges

Natalie's biggest challenge is a one-word answer: "paperwork." • "Sometimes the day-to-day tasks get a little old."

Steps to Current Job

- University of North Carolina at Greensboro; Bachelor of Science in Early Childhood Education.
- University of North Carolina at Chapel Hill, coursework in barrier island ecology and geology.
- Elementary school teacher for 15 years.
- Guilford Technical Community College, Paramedic Certification.
- Paramedic for four years.

Advice

"This profession is extremely physically intensive. You are doing a lot of lifting of equipment, of people, of stretchers. You need to really be in good physical shape." Natalie says that although more women are entering this profession, it is still a male-dominated one. "Sometimes there are some 'old-school' males who don't feel that females should be in this position, given the physical nature of the work; and you need to let people know that you're there to do a job, you're capable of doing the job. If you treat them like equals, generally, they look at you as an equal."

"You have to know who you are. It's going to take some experience. You grow into yourself. You have to have a good idea of what your likes are, what your dislikes are. Take a hard look at yourself, know what your strengths are, what your weaknesses are. You're going to make mistakes. You're going to find yourself in situations where you say, 'What the heck am I doing?' It's only from those situations that you know what to do next time." Natalie also says, "wherever you think you're going in life, whatever little mapped plan you have in your head, use it as a guide only because the directions are going to change, and if you are so locked into that plan… you're going to make yourself miserable. Look at any kind of change or misfortune as an opportunity to change direction or take another path. Be willing to look in that other direction, and you're going to have a happy existence."

Helpful Personality Traits

Ability to work with a variety of different personalities, level-headed, good communicator, strong stomach, and empathetic.

Hobbies & Interests

Reading Southern fiction, mystery, and nature books; doing crafts; singing; and photography.

Natalie also works as the executive director for the Cape Lookout Environmental Education Center, a nonprofit organization that she founded 10 years ago. For more information, go to www.cleec.org.

Pam Van Dyk

Education Research Consultant

{ *"I've always loved working with people, and I've always loved numbers, and this is a perfect combination of the two."* }

Job Description

Pam says, "I provide research design and planning for educational institutions and more frequently nonprofit organizations that focus on child and family services." She goes on to explain, "We try and help them understand what sort of impact they're having on their participants in a standardized way."

A Day on the Job

Touches base with her two employees, usually by e-mail. "I have a virtual office. I have employees, but I don't have an office that we all come to… and they manage projects just like I do, so I always try and make sure they don't need anything from me." • Conducts site visits to programs that she is evaluating. • Observes the program's participants in action and takes notes. • Interviews the program's staff. • Administers "pre" and "post" tests. For example, if Pam is evaluating a teen-parenting program, she says, "we might be administering a test when they enter the program to see what their attitudes towards parenting are; and we might go back [in the spring] and do a post test to see if those attitudes have changed." • Analyzes data that she and her employees gather from tests, interviews, and observations. "We use statistical software programs to do that. If we're doing an observation, and I'm writing three pages of notes, when I type them, I might cut and paste into a software program that will allow me later to look for themes and trends and things that I might not see." Pam also does a lot of analysis of demographics and test scores where the statistics show her themes and trends. Pam explains, "when we run the statistics, it will tell us [for example] is there a significant difference between how males and females perform in this program." • Writes reports and journal articles on her findings.

Job Likes

"I like being self-employed. I like the autonomy and the flexibility." • "I've always loved working with people, and I've always loved numbers, and this is a perfect combination of the two; and you don't get that opportunity very often."

• "I feel good about what I'm doing. I'm helping programs to do better work so that their participants have better outcomes."

Job Challenges

"There isn't a lot I don't like about my job," but because she works for herself, Pam says, "I don't always like being ultimately responsible for all decisions. Sometimes it would be nice to have someone else make them for me."

Steps to Current Job

• Western Washington University, Bellingham, Washington; Bachelor of Arts in Human Services. Pam was a preschool teacher for two years during this time.
• Owner/operator of a preschool for three years. During this time, Pam worked on her master's degree.
• North Carolina State University in Raleigh, Masters in Public Administration with a concentration in Nonprofit Management. Did an internship in program evaluation that led to her first consulting job.
• North Carolina State University, Raleigh; Doctorate in Education Research and Evaluation. Pam worked as an independent consultant while working on both her master's and Ph.D. and continues to do so.

Advice

Pam thinks that a good undergraduate degree for this field is one in social sciences (for example, sociology, psychology, social services, or human services). She says, "those undergraduate degrees give you the basics, and you really should plan on a master's degree." In addition, Pam says that anyone who wants to pursue a career like hers has to "be a curious person who really likes to read and study about a lot of different things."

"You have to set goals—early, even when you're in high school. You have to be thinking, 'What do I want to be doing in five years?' and you have to work towards that—even if the path is crooked." Pam doesn't assume that you have to figure it all out while you're in high school, and says, "you can't know while you're in high school what you want to do for the rest of your life. You might change your mind a lot, but when you set out to do something, it's really a good idea to finish. I think it helps you feel like you can accomplish something if you can just finish what you start."

Helpful Personality Traits

Curious, questioning, like to read and write, and interested in mathematics and technology.

Hobbies & Interests
Reading everything—nonfiction, mysteries, newspapers, magazines; playing guitar; music; swimming; running and learning new things. "I consider that a hobby. Lately, my new thing is mathematics, mathematicians, and the history of mathematics."

Paula Stewart

Veterinarian

{ *"Animals require a lot of trust and caring because they are usually scared or nervous and do not understand why they are sick."* }

Job Description
Paula is a medical doctor who provides medical and preventative care to domestic animals. She works at an animal hospital.

A Day on the Job
Starts the day making rounds with the overnight veterinarian to learn about newly admitted patients and to check on her overnight patients. • Assesses current patients. • Reviews files of scheduled patients. • Sees scheduled appointments for preventive care or specific problems—"anything from first puppy or kitten checkups, to yearly exams and vaccinations, to specific problems like an eye infection, cough, or arthritis." • Two-hour break for lunch and to check on current patients, to inform owners of their pets' progress, and to perform procedures such as biopsies, X rays, and so on. • Ends the day making rounds with the night doctor to update him or her on the status of overnight patients.

Job Likes
Veterinary medicine combines Paula's love for animals and people. "It allows me to work with animals, which I definitely love. Animals require a lot of trust and caring because they are usually scared or nervous and do not understand why they are sick. I also have to be compassionate and understanding with the people who bring their pets to see me. Since the animals cannot talk to you, in veterinary medicine you spend a lot of time talking to the animal's caretakers. This can be very rewarding because you not only have a relationship with your animal patients, you also have a connection with people in the community." • She

enjoys "piecing together the puzzle" of her patients' problems. "The dog or cat can't tell you what's wrong; it's a mystery. You really have to piece it together by asking the owners questions and dwelling into what the problem could be." • "There's a public health aspect to it that makes me feel like I'm contributing to the overall health of the people in my community." • "I work with a lot of other veterinarians, and I'm in an environment where I am constantly able to continue learning. It keeps me sharper." • "There's a lot of job opportunity, which prevents burnout." Some examples of other areas where veterinarians could focus are surgery, research, pharmaceuticals, or public health.

Job Challenges

Owners sometimes decide not to pursue treatment for their pet largely for financial reasons. It is frustrating for Paula to have the knowledge and resources to heal a patient, only to have the owner decide not to proceed with treatment. • "Sometimes I wish I could just treat the animals and not have to worry about the business aspect of things." Dealing with clients is sometimes difficult because they can be very emotionally attached to their animals. • "It can be a struggle to convince people to trust you with their pet." People tend to question the recommended treatments of animals more often than they would question their own medical doctor.

Steps to Current Job

- North Carolina State University in Raleigh; Bachelor of Science in *Zoology* with a concentration in Pre-Med.
- Research in the pathology department at the University of North Carolina at Chapel Hill with hemophilic dogs for three years.
- North Carolina State University in Raleigh; Doctor of Veterinary Medicine (DVM). During summer breaks, Paula did a fellowship in lab-animal medicine at Emory University in Atlanta, Georgia, and a veterinary-leadership program at Cornell University in Ithaca, New York.
- Internship at a small-animal private practice for one year.
- Associate veterinarian at a different small-animal private practice for one year.
- Associate veterinarian at a small-animal private practice—the same practice where she interned.

Advice

"Study hard. You definitely have to have good grades and be consistent in your grades." But Paula also thinks, "it's important to have some experience with animals to show that you've thought about what you want to do and have researched it." She says that you can get this experience by working or volunteering at a veterinarian's office. In college, try to get research experience—

"something to show that scientifically you understand that aspect of veterinary medicine. Veterinary schools are really looking for someone who is well-rounded as far as having hands-on experience with animals and dealing with clients, but also well-rounded with being able to read scientific papers and understand how science itself works."

"It's important to have a goal and never give up on that goal, but at the same time when you are striving for one goal, a lot of doors may open along the way that may show another goal that's even better. Keep an open mind." Paula's original goal was medical school, but as she worked in the research job at UNC-Chapel Hill trying to get experience for medical school, she realized that veterinary school was the place for her. Another bit of advice Paula learned from experience is to realize that "everyone is supposed to be at a different place in their life at a different time." While she was in veterinary school, she had to overcome the feeling that she was being left behind because her friends were getting jobs and starting families and she was still in school.

Helpful Personality Traits
People skills, compassion, patience, enjoy life sciences, business skills, and enjoy problem solving.

Hobbies & Interests
Outdoor activities including hiking, horseback riding, and jogging with her dog; reading; socializing with friends; and meeting new people.

> *Zoology* is the scientific study of the biology of animals.

Pegi Follachio

General Contractor

> "*A general contractor is to building as a conductor is to running an orchestra.*"

Job Description
Pegi oversees every aspect of building or remodeling a structure from start to finish. She communicates the ideas of architects, designers, and building owners to

subcontractors or to her own crew, and then manages each project until the entire job is complete. Most of Pegi's projects are residential properties, but she does some commercial and historical work. She specializes in kitchens and bathrooms. "I decided to target a market that I felt was recession-proof."

A Day on the Job
Starts early around 6:30 a.m. by checking e-mails, returning phone calls, and clearing her desk. • Checks existing jobs by meeting with subcontractors and visiting job sites. Pegi usually has about six projects going at a time. "For example, tomorrow I am meeting with my marble man to do templates for all the marble fireplaces that we are doing on one job." • Meets with architects, clients, and potential clients to discuss current or future projects—"looking over their plans and talking to them about what they want." • Studies blueprints and design ideas to determine plans for subcontractors. • Puts together bids for potential projects.

Job Likes
"It is creatively challenging. It's a lot of problem-solving." • "I love seeing the finished product... and seeing the excitement with the client." Many of her client relationships grow into friendships. • "I love the organizational part of it." • "I love working with men. There are very few women in this business." Pegi finds the men she works with "direct and concrete thinkers." • It is fun for Pegi to draw blueprints and renderings by hand, because she likes that it is a way to communicate visually.

Job Challenges
For every job, a permit is required. There is a lot of waiting, politics, and red tape that come with "pulling permits" in the city of Atlanta. • The final walk-through with the client on a job site, known as "punch out," is not always smooth because some clients are very hard to please.

Steps to Current Job
- Brenau College for Women in Gainesville, Georgia; Bachelor of Arts in English.
- University of North Carolina at Chapel Hill, Master of Arts in English.
- High school and college English teacher; middle school gifted teacher for 15 years.
- Managed the redesign of a suite for a national convention, which sparked her interest in general contracting.
- Took contracting courses at Georgia Tech in Atlanta.
- Passed the residential contractor's certification exam.
- General contractor for small jobs and worked underneath another general contractor to gain experience for four years.

- Owner of a *sheet-rocking* and painting business.
- General contractor. Pegi owns one of the largest female-owned general contracting businesses in Atlanta.

Advice

"Spend your summers interning with a general contractor to see if it is something you like." Pegi also says "I think it's really, really important that they love detail work, because this is a very detail-oriented job. In fact, on my bids that I give, I always have at the bottom of it, 'God is in the details.'"

Pegi believes that a liberal arts degree is very beneficial. "There is nothing like liberal arts because it teaches you to think, and it allows you to be very expansive." What you learn from a liberal-arts degree—aspects such as people skills and psychology—are just as important as being able to draw blueprints or being able to do the math for a bid.

Helpful Personality Traits

Organized, creative, good communicator, hardworking, and mathematically competent.

Hobbies & Interests

Reading, hiking, snow skiing, and drumming.

Subcontractors are hired to complete a job in their particular specialties. Examples of subcontractors include roofers, electricians, and plumbers.

Sheet rock is a kind of plasterboard that is used to make the smooth surface of interior house walls. It's also known as drywall.

NO PATH IS SET IN STONE

It is important to have goals. Donna Helms, the golf professional, even advises that you write them down. But don't let your end goal keep you from making diversions that might teach you things about yourself. Veterinarian Paula Stewart wanted to be a medical doctor, but a research project using dogs piqued her interest in veterinary science. Had Paula disregarded that impulse, she might be a frustrated medical doctor now. Keep your eyes on your original goal, but be open to new adventures that might ultimately change your direction.

Polly Leousis

Manager of a Corporate Foundation

{ *"I love the fact that most of my work is around physical activity and nutrition because that's a personal interest of mine."* }

Job Description

Polly works for her company's foundation and funds programs that promote health and wellness. A foundation is a legal organization that distributes funds to *nonprofit* organizations that align with its focus areas. Polly's foundation is funded by a donation from her company, so she and her co-workers do not have to raise money. They draw from the interest earned on the original donation's investments.

In addition to determining which nonprofits will receive grants, Polly also works with her department to create signature community health programs. As she says, "We not only give grants, we also develop programs in areas where we see a need in the community."

A Day on the Job

Reviews grant proposals and makes recommendations for funding. • Helps educate nonprofit organizations about the foundation, its focus areas, eligibility requirements, and application processes. • Works on contracts with grantees, "…to make sure that they're clearly stating what the grant will be used for and how programs will be evaluated." • Manages and implements the company's signature community health programs, "trying to ensure that they're meeting a community need and running smoothly."

Job Likes

"There are so many things I like about my job." • "The ability to be creative. I love to be able to brainstorm and try to create solutions to meet community needs." • "I love the fact that most of my work is around physical activity and nutrition because that's a personal interest of mine." • "I have the best team that I have ever worked with in my whole life. They're great, smart, and very professional. They know how to balance having a good time at work, but they also know how to get the work done. Having a strong team is critical if you want to be successful in the workplace."

Job Challenges
"Sometimes it's frustrating not having the resources to fund more programs."

Steps to Current Job
- Longwood College, Farmville, Virginia; Bachelor of Science in Sociology with a Criminal Justice Application.
- Sorority consultant, 10 months (traveled across the country teaching different chapters of her sorority how to operate efficiently).
- Administrative work for a motorcycle dealership for one and a half years.
- Temp work for one year.
- Administrative work for the North Carolina Department of Health and Human Services for six months.
- Training Coordinator for the Workforce Development Training Institute within the North Carolina Department of Commerce for two years.
- Coordinator for the Wake County JobLink Career Center for two and a half years.
- Director for the Governor's Work First Business Council within the North Carolina Department of Commerce for one year.
- University of North Carolina at Chapel Hill, Master of Science in Public Health. Polly worked on this degree while at her current job.
- Manager in a corporate foundation.

Advice
Before obtaining her current position, Polly helped people find jobs, and she says, "One of the best things you can do when you're looking for any job, whether it's one in my field or another, is interest interviews—going to meet with people and not saying, 'Can I have a job,' but asking, 'How did you get into this? What do you like about it? What don't you like about it? Can you look at my resume? Can you give me any feedback on it?' It's one of the smartest things you can ever do. It helps you learn about the position, and it gives you perspective on whether your skills are a good match for the position."

When it comes to personal relationships, Polly says, "surround yourself with people who have your best interests at heart. That might be your parents, your sister, or it might just be friends—friends who really value all of your unique qualities. You'll find that you start to choose friends who say, 'I like you just the way you are.'"

Helpful Personality Traits
Collaborative, understanding of how nonprofit organizations work, good listener, intuitive, detail oriented, honest, have integrity, and creative.

Hobbies & Interests

Being physically active (Polly teaches fitness classes part time), spending time with family and friends, reading fiction, and singing.

> A *nonprofit* is an organization established for charitable, educational, or humanitarian purposes and not for making money.

Rebecca Schmorr

Dentist

{ *"When they come in for their checkups six months later, they have learned to smile real big. That's rewarding."* }

Job Description

Rebecca is a dentist and says her job is "to make sure that people have healthy teeth," but her focus is cosmetic dentistry. She has a staff of two hygienists who clean teeth and an assistant who directly assists her during procedures such as filling cavities, placing tooth implants, bleaching teeth, and preparing teeth for crowns and veneers.

A Day on the Job

Rebecca's day is typically from 8:30 a.m. to 5:30 p.m. Tuesday through Thursday. On Fridays, she works until 4:00 p.m. without a lunch break so that she can get a head start on her weekend. • Greets patients. • Performs "hygiene checks"—examines each patient's teeth after hygienists have cleaned them. • Talks with patients. "I alleviate their fears. I tell them what we're going to do." • Gives patients an injection to make their mouth numb if the procedure requires it. • Performs scheduled procedures on patients. Rebecca can do anywhere between 4 and 10 procedures a day, with 4 to 8 hygiene checks in between.

Job Likes

"It's very flexible. You're your own boss, so you choose how much or how little you want to work and how much or how little you want to make. There's complete autonomy." • "Yeah, we do a lot of drilling and filling," but Rebecca says that she also gives people smiles that they're proud of. "When they come in for their check ups six months later, they have learned to smile real big. That's rewarding."

Job Challenges

"They don't teach us in dental school how to run a small business, and that's what we do."

Steps to Current Job

- University of North Carolina at Chapel Hill. "I was an English major for about a year and a half. I didn't do very well, didn't take it seriously."
- Alamance Beauty College, Burlington, North Carolina; certification to cut and style hair.
- Hairdresser for five years. Rebecca moved to Indiana and says, "I decided to take some classes, did a lot better the second time around than I did the first time around. As much as I loved doing hair, when I told people I was a hairdresser, I always felt like I had to add a descriptor, 'yeah, but I'm really smart.'"
- Indiana University, Bloomington; finished science requirements necessary to attend dental school. Surprisingly, it isn't necessary to have a bachelor's degree to attend many dental schools; however, most recommend it. If you're interested in dentistry, be sure to check the requirements you'll need to get accepted to dental school.
- Indiana University School of Dentistry, Indianapolis; Doctor of Dental Surgery (D.D.S.).
- Dentist.

Advice

Rebecca says if you want to be a dentist, "don't sweat the small stuff in school, just get the grades because... what you learn and what you reap afterwards so outweigh the difficulties of school." Being a dentist requires purchasing lots of expensive equipment, and Rebecca admits that there are a lot of fads in dentistry. She, like a lot of other dentists, is a self-admitted gadget hound. "I wish that I had not jumped in and bought equipment before I had really found out enough about it." Surprisingly, Rebecca thinks women pursuing dentistry should work out and keep a strong back because the job requires a lot of bending over. "We naturally have such weak backs... you've gotta go to the gym."

"Don't worry too much about what people think about you because those sorts of stresses go by so quickly." Rebecca says that if you're so eager to please your peers, "...it overwhelms almost every decision you make. Just get it in your head that pleasing your peers doesn't matter. Focus on being yourself and doing what feels right to you."

Helpful Personality Traits

Like to meet people and talk to people, empathetic, flexible, and let things "roll off."

Hobbies & Interests

Reading science fiction, gardening, travel, fine dining, and taking care of her animals.

Rebecca V. St. Jean

Optometrist and Business Owner

{ *"Eyes are sometimes called the windows to our health."* }

Job Description

Rebecca is an *optometrist* and the owner of an optometry practice. An optometrist is an eye doctor, someone who "ensures the health of the eyes and healthy vision. It's kind of like your family physician, but just for the eye." Usually when someone thinks of an optometrist, glasses and contact lenses come to mind. Although this is a big part of Rebecca's job, it is interesting to point out that Rebecca is also able to detect and observe problems within the body. "Eyes are sometimes called the windows to our health. Any vascular disease that damages blood vessels (hypertension, high cholesterol, diabetes, and so on) can be detected during an eye exam. Also, neurological disease processes can be picked up, such as multiple sclerosis, AIDS, sarcoidosis, and so on, because those diseases' processes also affect the nerves of the eye."

A Day on the Job

Four out of five days are patient-care days. Each day, she conducts about 20 annual eye exams, usually corrective lens checkups, and about 10 to 15 problem-related exams—"injuries, infections, glaucoma, things like that." • The fifth day is an administrative day where Rebecca attends to the business aspect of running her optometry practice. • Every day requires practice management to ensure that her practice is running smoothly and that her staff of five has the supplies they need. For example, "right now, we're having a software problem with our computer system, and I'm dealing with a vendor on that."

Job Likes
"It's one of the few health professions that I get to deal with well patients rather than sick patients." • "I get to interact with people every day." Rebecca learned from her first job out of undergraduate school, an environmental research position, that she wanted more interaction with a variety of people. • As a small-business owner, "I can set my own hours." • "I enjoy the aspect of helping people." • Continuing education is required each year and Rebecca enjoys the learning process.

Job Challenges
For the most part, Rebecca enjoys her patients, but there is that "two percent of the time that we don't seem to meet the expectations of a patient." • "That's the advantage and disadvantage [of being a small-business owner]. I just walked in the door from doing some stuff at the office even though the office is closed."

Steps to Current Job
- George Washington University in Washington, D.C.; Bachelor of Science with a double major in Biology and Environmental Science and a minor in Physics; member of the swim team.
- Environmental research position for approximately one year.
- Southern College in Memphis, Tennessee; Doctor of Optometry.
- Optional residency at a hospital for one year.
- Worked at an *ophthalmologist's* office for two years.
- Optometrist and owner of an optometry office.

Advice
Rebecca would advise against getting an undergraduate degree in a pre-optometry program, because if you discover midway through school that you don't like optometry, you'll have to start all over. "I tell them basically to get a degree in something that interests them, but to be sure they have those core courses that are required [for graduate schools]." She also encourages young women to talk or work with their local optometrist to make sure that this is the career for them.

Many graduate students accumulate large student loans, and Rebecca says, "I wish I had considered the military a little bit more because it is an alternative way to finance an advanced degree."

Helpful Personality Traits
Strong interest or aptitude for science and math and good people skills.

Hobbies & Interests
Swimming, charity work, and involved with her church.

An *optometrist* and an *ophthalmologist* both perform eye exams and prescribe glasses or contact lenses. The difference between the two is that an ophthalmologist is a surgeon who performs eye surgeries and also treats eye diseases. An ophthalmologist must complete medical school and a required number of years in internships and residencies before he or she can practice.

Richelle Fox

Personal Trainer and Fitness Consultant

{ *"It's the satisfaction of helping them reach their goals and go beyond."* }

Job Description
"I basically help people reach their fitness and health goals in creative ways." Richelle devises a fitness plan specific to each client, and using various exercises and equipment, she helps them get their bodies in shape. Richelle's extensive swimming background and education have taught her many "creative ways" to assist people in reaching their physical goals. As a fitness consultant, Richelle is hired to give advice and direction or to present a program for a specific purpose. For example, local swim teams might ask her to devise a dry-land program for their swimmers.

A Day on the Job
Assesses her client's current physical condition and then devises a training program specific to his or her needs and goals. "I focus on core strength, stabilization work, postural assessments, and figuring out what their deficiencies and imbalances are in their bodies to begin with... before we move on to strengthening, weight loss, or whatever their primary goals are." • Usually conducts five one-hour, one-on-one training sessions—either at a gym or in her client's home. • Long-term clients require periodic evaluation to update their programs.

Job Likes
Richelle likes "motivating others to reach their goals and see them successful. It's the satisfaction of helping them reach their goals and go beyond." • "It's great to see how much you can help people." • Richelle enjoys attending continuing-education meetings in major cities throughout the United States. She finds the speakers "amazing to listen to."

Job Challenges
When she works as a personal trainer for a gym, the early morning schedule is not her favorite. Besides that, Richelle really can't think of anything else she doesn't like!

Steps to Current Job
- University of California at Los Angeles; studied physiological sciences for two years, member of the varsity swim team.
- Member of the Resident National Swim Team training for the 1996 Olympics at the Olympic Training Center in Colorado Springs, Colorado.
- University of North Carolina at Chapel Hill; Bachelor of Arts in Physical Education with an emphasis in Exercise Science; captain of the varsity swim team.
- Trained for the 2000 Olympic Trials for a year and a half. Richelle's swimming credentials include gold medals in the 1997 and 1999 Pan Pacific Championships, a gold medal in the 1998 Goodwill Games, and a U.S. National title in 1996.
- Earned her personal trainer certification from the National Academy of Sports Medicine (for more information, see www.nasm.org). She also has a pre- and post-natal certification from the American Aerobic Association International (www.aaai-ismafitness.com).
- Personal trainer for a well-known sports club.
- Personal trainer/fitness consultant and women's wellness center owner. As a women's fitness and wellness center owner, Richelle is currently involved in managing the gym, expanding the programs, and training the personal trainers.

Advice
"It's definitely an advantage to have some kind of an education or background in exercise science; some kind of anatomy or physiology background. You'd want to get as many certifications and specialty certifications as possible... whether it's the senior population, pre- and post-natal, post-rehab, anything like that. The more certifications you have, the better off you are going to be."

Richelle is inspired by John Norley's quote, "All things are difficult before they are easy." She believes that you should "challenge yourself, be disciplined, work hard, set realistic goals, and you'll live your dreams."

Helpful Personality Traits
Confident, motivator, enjoy working with people, willing to be a role model by leading a healthy lifestyle, a good listener, patient, good communicator, friendly, and disciplined.

Hobbies & Interests

Physical activities, running races, triathlons, spending time with family, watching movies, and people-watching.

Ronda Capps

Flight Attendant

{ *"It's an excellent way to get out there to see the country and the world."* }

Job Description

A flight attendant works on an airplane and is responsible for the safety and the comfort of the airplane's passengers.

A Day on the Job

Ronda is a commuter. "I fly to work. I don't live where my trip starts." • After arriving at the airport, she boards the plane on which she will be working. Ronda starts her flight on the East Coast and usually finishes that day's flight on the West Coast. • Makes sure that all safety equipment is in place and working and that catering supplies (for serving meals) are full. "The first thing I do is look at all of the safety equipment on the airplane." • Greets the passengers when they board the plane. • Performs a safety demonstration for the passengers. • Serves refreshments and attends to passengers' needs. • Stays overnight in her destination city and prepares for a return flight the next day.

Job Likes

"It's an excellent way to get out there to see the country and the world." • Ronda enjoys her flexible schedule. "Everyone has his or her own idea of what schedule is good for them," and after working for the same airline for a while, a flight attendant can decide his or her own schedule and flight destinations. Now that Ronda has a small child, her schedule of working three or four days a week has its advantages. • Ronda feels a camaraderie with her fellow flight attendants. "There are not a lot of jobs where you work with the same people for 18 years."

Job Challenges

Being away from her young child is difficult. • "Dealing with people that are angry or frustrated."

Steps to Current Job
- Clemson University, Clemson, South Carolina; Bachelor of Arts in Political Science.
- Flight attendant.

Advice
Being a flight attendant is an excellent job to start with because it allows you to see your country and the world, meet new people, and learn about different cultures. Ronda also sees her job as a good first job because it can be a "stepping stone" in your career path. Just think, when you are in a job interview, you can say that you have experience in customer service, emergency situations, and working with a variety of people; are well-traveled; and have a knowledge of different cultures.

"You should follow your instincts. What you think you are good at, follow that because you are probably great at it."

Helpful Personality Traits
Patient, outgoing, and a professional attitude.

Hobbies & Interests
Running and antiquing.

Sandie Salvaggio-Walker

General Manager for a Community Orchestra and Voice Instructor*

"As long as people stand and applaud, you know you've done your job."

Job Description
Known as "Symphony Sandie" around town, Sandie manages the tasks of running a community symphony orchestra. She coordinates six concerts per year and community educational programs. Sandie also assists the symphony board members with their committee tasks.

Sandie Salvaggio-Walker, general manager for a community orchestra, greets a concertgoer.

A Day on the Job

Attends to office duties, such as returning calls, checking e-mail, opening mail, and so on. • Applies for grants to fund the symphony. • Solicits for advertisements and sponsors. She works with the development committee to find people to donate money to the symphony. • Speaks publicly to inform the community about the symphony. • Coordinates symphony brochures and concert programs for each concert. • Makes arrangements for the guest artists. Sandie handles their contracts, makes hotel and travel arrangements, rents any instruments needed (for example, a grand piano), and attends to the artists' needs while they are in town. • Reserves the venues for each concert. • Educates the local youth by organizing symphonic programs. Sandie runs a young artist competition that allows the winner to play with the symphony orchestra. She also coordinates third- and sixth-grade orchestra appreciation education. • Works the concerts. This includes ticketing, greeting guests, passing out programs, and clean-up. • Assists the reception committee with coordinating receptions that follow each concert. • Plans various budgets. • Maintains permanent files about the history of the Hendersonville Symphony Orchestra.

---

*Sandie has taught voice lessons out of her home for 38 years. She teaches all ages and averages about 10 students per year. "The love of music is what I'd like to instill in them." Sandie feels that she has made a difference in her students' lives by teaching them an appreciation for the art. "My students know what it is to get up on stage and perform. They appreciate the art of singing." She also enjoys lifelong relationships with many of them.

Job Likes

"I'm not that much of a classical musician, but I love music. I'm working with musicians all the time." • "I love all we do for education and teaching young people that symphonies can be fun. It doesn't have to be high-brow." *Carnival of the Animals* is a favorite for third-graders. • "I feel honored to work for an organization that is so dedicated." Sandie reports to a working board of volunteers, which means that each board member chairs or participates on a committee. • Sandie likes the freedom of her hours. She is a part-time employee and is not held to a strict hourly schedule. "The reason I can be part-time is that I have a working board." Not all general manager/executive director positions are part-time.

Job Challenges

Sandie reports to a board of 25 people and says, "It's challenging to work for 25 personalities." • "The biggest orchestras have the same problem as the smallest orchestras. How can we attract people to come to our concerts and pay to come and hear classical music? That is a universal problem." Sandie feels that most Americans are not brought up learning to appreciate classical music. • Working for a small, community symphony orchestra, the pay is minimal. • It's difficult for the board to know all that goes into making a program run smoothly.

Steps to Current Job

- Montreat Anderson College in Montreat, North Carolina; general college and business courses.
- North Carolina School of the Arts in Winston-Salem; studied voice and piano.
- Full-time mother for 17 years. She held part-time jobs throughout this time.
- Full-time receptionist for doctors' offices for 10 years.
- General manager for a symphony orchestra.

Advice

Concerning education, Sandie says that studying music administration or business would be helpful for her position. She points out that the more education you have, the higher salary you can command. Although being a musician is helpful to Sandie in her position, it is not a requirement. She also suggests investigating the American Symphony Orchestra League. They have an Orchestra Management Fellowship Program, and they also provide seminars that assist general managers/executive directors of symphonies and orchestras.

"Do something that you like. That doesn't necessarily mean you are going to make a lot of money. The quality of your life is going to be better. You will feel good about yourself."

Helpful Personality Traits
Outgoing, fun, gracious, and humble.

Hobbies & Interests
Singing, reading, golf, and walking.

"To thine own self be true."

—William Shakespeare

Sandra Canfield

International Development Resource Coordinator for Nonprofit Organization

{ *"I love the fact that I'm hopefully leaving this world a better place than when I came into it."* }

Job Description
Sandra works for RTI International, a company that is contracted by donors (often the U.S. government) to assist developing countries in better managing their educational, health, and governmental systems. This is often called international development, and Sandra's job presently is to locate technical experts that are a good match for specific projects in fields such as HIV, primary education and curriculum development, and municipal management.

A Day on the Job
Receives internal requests that identify technical experts for proposals. "Basically, the donor says, 'We need help in providing a certain service to a certain country' and then requests firms to put together bids for services. We propose experts to carry out the work." • Looks through curriculum vitae (CVs, or resumes) of prospective experts. Many prospects are already in foreign countries. Sandra

stresses, "Young women should make sure they put together a strong CV. Networking is the best way to learn about opportunities." • Makes recommendations for proposing candidates to bid on proposals. • Helps write proposals. "We help put together multimillion-dollar proposals… this is big stuff. It's a lot of pressure. • Travels to developing countries when necessary for research. At the time of her interview, Sandra had recently returned from Indonesia and is always prepared to travel again in the future.

Job Likes

"I love the fact that I'm hopefully leaving this world a better place than when I came into it." • Sandra likes that she gets to see many different cultures. "Some people could take the worst of each place, but I try to look at what each place has to offer."

Job Challenges

"It's hard to go to these countries and see… poverty like you've never seen it before. It's hard to go to war-torn countries and see hate like you've never seen it before." • "It's hard being in a country when you don't have family and friends and you don't speak the language." • "It's hard to have a career that not a lot of people understand."

Steps to Current Job
- Villanova University, Pennsylvania; Bachelor of Arts in Psychology.
- American University, Washington D.C.; Master of International Affairs.
- Media and non-governmental organization (NGO) liaison for a United Nations specialized agency, International Fund for Agricultural Development (IFAD), for one year.
- Operations analyst, contractor, for the World Bank for one and a half years.
- Acting country program assistant, contractor, for the World Bank for one year.
- Program manager for humanitarian assistance in Kosovo with Catholic Relief Services for one year.
- Program manager for monetization and food security with Catholic Relief Services in Burkina Faso, Africa, for nine months.
- Resource coordinator for RTI International.

Advice

"Foreign-language skills are really important." Sandra recommends learning one of the "major" languages, such as French, Spanish, or Arabic. "Internships are fabulous because they really put you in a good position to get that first job. I had about five. They teach you how to behave in a workplace." Sandra says that it is very difficult, without putting in a lot of years, to be in a management position in this field without a master's degree, but if she could take different steps on her career path, she thinks, "I would have probably gone back and found a skill or expertise that I was really passionate about and then applied that skill to my overseas work. I would recommend that people get their undergraduate degrees, explore career-wise and skill-wise what they want to do, and then go back and get their master's." Sandra also says, "Young women will need to decide whether or not they want to live and work overseas in third-world, developing countries or whether they can satisfy their career goals and interests in the U.S. or other international hub, such as Geneva, Brussels, or Nairobi."

Recognize that you have strength and skills, and don't second-guess yourself too much, Sandra says. She also thinks that it's a good idea to learn more about world politics. "People here [in the U.S.] take things for granted—the freedoms and liberties we have."

Helpful Personality Traits
Curiosity, balance between idealism and realism (what should be and what is), flexible, and tough, both mentally and physically.

Hobbies & Interests
Culture, experiencing ethnic cuisines, and outdoor activities.

Shannon Hall

Freelance Makeup Artist, Wardrobe Stylist, and Set Designer for Photo and Film/Video Shoots and Live Events

{ *"I think the best title for me, my daughter gave me in the second grade. When she was asked what I did, she said, 'I think she's a make-it-up artist.' That fits me best. I make it up everyday."* }

Job Description
"I am a creative resource for getting what other people want done visually." Because Shannon is working in a smaller market, she is often asked to do all of her roles—makeup, wardrobe, and sets—for any given project. In larger markets, such as New York City or Los Angeles, there is only one person assigned to each of these tasks.

"Make-it-up" artist Shannon Hall takes a break on the set.

A Day on the Job

Arrives on a production prepared for any situation "…because I'm working with other creative people that have ideas of their own. So I show up, and I've got an idea, or I'm prepared to take their idea and make it happen." • If Shannon is acting as a wardrobe stylist or a set designer, she will discuss with the director or photographer what "look" they are trying to obtain. The script and her conversations with the director/photographer are key to her selections of clothing and props. • If Shannon is hired as a set designer, she will arrange all of the furniture and accessories necessary to visually communicate the director or photographer's vision. Sometimes she selects these items, but other times she has to work with what she's given. She remains on the set for the whole shoot to change things as necessary and handle any situations that might arise. • As a wardrobe stylist, Shannon selects all wardrobe and dresses the actors. Again she remains on the set for the entirety of the shoot. • If she is hired as a makeup artist, Shannon comes to the production with her extensive makeup kit and applies makeup to actors and sometimes styles their hair. • Bills clients for her services.

Job Likes

"I like that it's creative. The more creative, the better." • "I like being able to make something out of nothing, and I like having an idea and seeing it to fruition. Then I like seeing the end product. It's fun to be in a grocery store, pick up a magazine, and show my mom something I did."

Job Challenges

Because Shannon is a freelancer, her work ebbs and flows. "It not being steady allows me to live my life and to be there for my daughter… it not being steady also means my money's not steady."

Steps to Current Job

- College of Charleston, South Carolina; studied psychology for one year.
- Moved to New York City. "I thought I was going to be a movie star, I thought I was going to be a rock star."
- Freelance photographer assistant: styling sets, preparing wardrobes.
- Personal assistant to pop singer Cyndi Lauper for one year.
- Wardrobe stylist to Cyndi Lauper for *True Colors* tour.
- Wardrobe stylist for the Monkees reunion tour.
- Freelance "make-it-up artist" for 16 years—recently she has worked on many fashion shoots with Olympic gold medalist Marion Jones.

Advice

"I think anybody who wants to pursue a career like this needs to move to a city for a while and work as an assistant. Assist somebody in makeup. Assist somebody in wardrobe. Just intern, assist. If you just start going into studios and talking to people, you'll make the connections." Shannon also thinks that it's important to go to school and get some kind of background in art, and she says the Fashion Institute of Technology in New York City has an excellent program for stylists. Although Shannon is quick to add, "*Not* having that education didn't give me any boundaries."

"Think of possibilities, not the impossibilities, and if there's something you want to do, go do it." Shannon also only slightly jokes, "Don't play with any boys." She says, "get some focus on what it is you want to do, and really, don't let anybody get in your way. If you get yourself focused on what your boyfriend wants to do or what your boyfriend wants *you* to do, or what your parents want you to do, then you're not living your life, but if you focus on what it is *you* want to do and don't take 'no' for an answer, you can do it! Just keep going."

Helpful Personality Traits

Creative, resourceful, and enthusiastic.

Hobbies & Interests

Working out, photography, art, yoga, throwing parties, and watching films.

Shelley Chafin

Nanny

{ *"Where else could you get a job where you get paid everyday to play?"* }

Shelley Chafin, a nanny, works on puzzles with Charlie and Erica.

Job Description

Shelley is the primary caregiver for a couple's two children while they are working. Unlike some nannies, Shelley has set hours from 8:30 a.m. until 5:30 p.m., weekdays, with the exception of Wednesday, when she stays until 10:30 p.m. to give the parents a "date night."

A Day on the Job

Unloads and loads the dishwasher while the mother plays with the kids. • Plays with the children together with the mother to make the transition of mom going to work less traumatic. "We have a pretty set schedule because I feel that it's easier for them [the children]." • Reads and plays with the children on her own.

• Plans some sort of outing with the children. "Today, we went and got Charlie's hair cut. Everybody got balloons and everybody got lollipops." • Makes lunch for the kids, but "we also eat lunch out quite a bit. One of Charlie's favorite places to go is Snoopy's. So today, we went and got hot dogs and brought them back here." • Puts the children down for their naps; does their laundry and takes out the trash while they're sleeping. • Changes the children's diapers when they wake up from their naps. • Makes an afternoon snack for the kids. • Plays with the children until their mother arrives home from work.

Job Likes

"I like the flexibility." Shelley has her own school-age children, and says, "I like that I can bring my kids with me if I want to bring them with me. I always call Jodi [the mother] as a consideration. I don't do it on a regular basis, but I like that a lot." • "I get paid really well. I have great benefits, great vacation. They got me a car." • "Where else could you get a job where you get paid everyday to play? In the summertime, you get to go to the pool. You get to travel."

Job Challenges

"Sometimes I have to bite my tongue." No two people have the same parenting styles, and it can be frustrating when Shelley's employers do things differently than she would.

Steps to Current Job

- Appalachian State University, Boone, North Carolina, for three and a half years. Shelley left to get married before she finished her degree, "which was stupid in hindsight."
- Stay-at-home mother for 11 years.
- Waitress for one and a half years.
- Secretary for six months.
- Nanny.

Advice

"I don't know any nannies that have been placed through agencies. Everybody I know has found their jobs through family and friends or the Internet, word of mouth." Once you get a job as a nanny, Shelley says, "you and the family have to fit. You have to have a lot of similar beliefs as far as how a child should be disciplined, how a child should be treated, how a child should learn, religious beliefs... you don't have to agree completely... but you have to be similar enough that what you're teaching is going to bleed over and what they're teaching is going to bleed over." Shelley also thinks that it's really important to be a good communicator. "Be upfront from the beginning. There's a lot that you need to establish from the get-go as far as your hours, your vacation."

Shelley believes that it is very important to "value yourself. You are a person that's articulate and smart and intelligent, and you should value your opinion, and don't be afraid to express it. Don't let yourself be defined by your boyfriend. You are your own person, with or without this person."

Helpful Personality Traits
Flexible because all children are different, pleasant, upbeat, and creative at getting tasks accomplished throughout the day.

Hobbies & Interests
Reading (anything and everything), spending time with her children and watching their sporting events (basketball and baseball).

Shelly Webb

College Chaplain

{ *"We can have these wonderful discussions that don't have God in a box, but has open-endedness, mystery."* }

Chaplain Shelly Webb preaches at a Baccalaureate service.

Job Description

"I serve mostly as a spiritual guide to the faculty, staff, and students." Shelly also organizes campus religious activities and programs and teaches one religion class a semester. She works for a small, private college that hosts a diverse group of religions. "I'm an ordained Christian minister, but I serve a community that is very diverse."

A Day on the Job

Counsels students seeking vocational direction. "They come and talk about where they feel led in life, when they're asking the God questions like 'What does God want me to do with my life?'" • Walks around campus making herself available to students. • Teaches one religion or faith-development class per semester. • Advises and supports religious-life groups on campus. • Meets with prospective students. • Leads religious retreats. • Represents the college at the United Methodist annual conference. • Acts as a liaison to local churches and plans the programs that the college students provide to them. • Organizes campus worship services. • Provides the prayer for campus ceremonies. "I call myself a professional pray-er." • Preaches throughout the state. • Attends crisis situations. "I'm the one that has to go to the hospital to meet the parents. It's one aspect that I don't enjoy necessarily, but I find it vitally important."

Job Likes

"My favorite part is meeting with the students and hearing their different perspectives on spirit and their dreams of what they want to do with their life." • "I love theological conversations. We can have these wonderful discussions that don't have God in a box, but have open-endedness, mystery. Just an open discussion." • "I enjoy worship with college students. It's oftentimes very creative. It's very folk style. It's around the campfire or by the creek... playing guitars or prayers that use a more common language that's relevant to 20-something-year-olds." • "I like the challenge of teaching classes. I find that when you teach a subject, you learn so much more. It stretches me personally." • "It's always fluid. There's change every year. There's no stagnant part about my job."

Job Challenges

The hours can be long. Shelly's responsibilities require her to work many nights and weekends. • "The administrative tasks are not fun, but essential if you're going to have a vibrant religious life program." • Sometimes students and people in the community do not validate a woman as a minister. "Just my being a woman sometimes discredits what I represent to that person... not to this college but to some individuals. I have to respect their theology."

Steps to Current Job
- Wofford College in Spartanburg, South Carolina; Bachelor of Arts in Sociology.
- Duke Divinity School in Durham, North Carolina; Master of Divinity. During this time, she became an ordained United Methodist minister.
- Associate pastor for a college church for four years.
- Pastor for a church for five years.
- College chaplain at Brevard College in North Carolina.

Advice
"I had to be basically talked into believing that women could serve as ministers because it's rare that you see women in the ministry. I never saw a woman minister. So the first thing I did was seek out those who were doing that, and I just went and talked to them." In high school, Shelly worked as a youth delegate at her church's annual conference, where she met and talked with women pastors. She also suggests looking in your phone book and calling women pastors in your area. Even though some of these women might not be the same denomination as you, Shelly thinks that the process is somewhat similar, and that the challenges women ministers face are universal. "You still feel that you have to do your job twice as good as a man to be accepted."

"Don't make barriers for yourself. Believe in your gifts and your skills. Find the people that support you." Shelly credits her dad for believing in her 100 percent and standing by her every step of the way. Having a positive support group helps you overcome your fears. "Fear can stymie you, and you can start believing that fear, too. Surround yourself with people that believe in you, and challenge those fears. Break it out!"

Helpful Personality Traits
Determined, creative, patient, confident, open-minded, open-hearted, sense of humor, good listener, and a good mediator.

Hobbies & Interests
Quilting, golf, hiking, music (Shelly plays the banjo and guitar), volleyball, and triathlons.

WOULD YOU CHANGE ANYTHING IF YOU COULD?

We were so surprised when the majority of women we interviewed said they wouldn't change a thing about their career paths. That's not to say that they didn't make mistakes or take the long way to get to their ultimate dream job. They now know that the potholes and the kinks in the road only helped them in figuring out their true desires and how to achieve them.

Don't worry if it seems like you're tripping or going the wrong way. In the process, you're going to stumble upon who you really are, and that is the ultimate goal.

Sujata Narayan Mody

Independent Organizational Development Consultant

"When it comes right down to it, it's not money that either keeps a person in a job or makes them leave, it's how they feel about who they can be in a job or whether or not they're valued."

Job Description

Sujata works with employees in organizations (from large corporations to small nonprofits) to help them create a workplace "that values every employee and enables them to work to their highest potential."

A Day on the Job

Reads policies and procedures of the companies that hire her. "I'm really trying to get a feel for what the organization is about. And, if what they say they are and what they're doing externally really matches up with what they say they are and what they're doing internally in terms of their employees." • Prepares needs assessments that outline areas in which an organization needs to improve. • Conducts phone meetings with executive management when necessary. "If there's some task that needs to be completed for the client, I might call up the client and we might have a conversation about it." • Conducts *focus groups* and one-on-one interviews with employees. • Shares findings through proposals, team-building sessions, and strategic planning sessions with employees and management.

Job Likes

"I love that I get to interact with people constantly." • "Being able to work with individuals to help them figure out what they need to really feel fulfilled in their work. That's pretty exciting for me." • "I love getting up and presenting and facilitating meetings—facilitating a team-building process." • Sujata enjoys learning about all different types of organizations (from art museums to companies that make soda).

Job Challenges

"Compiling all of the information and sitting down and trying to write it can be kind of a drag." • Because Sujata is an independent consultant, she's in and out of a lot of different companies, and it's sometimes hard to build relationships because, "you don't have that ongoing, continuous involvement. You're somewhat detached." • Not knowing whether the changes that Sujata suggests will be implemented can be frustrating to her.

Steps to Current Job

- University of North Carolina at Chapel Hill, Bachelor of Arts with a double major in Anthropology and International Studies.
- University of Michigan, Ann Arbor, Master of Urban Planning and Master of Science, Natural Resources and Environment.
- Workshop facilitator and researcher for one and a half years.
- Consulting associate for five months.
- Organizational/community change agent for two and a half years.
- Independent organizational development consultant.

Advice

Sujata doesn't think that this job requires a degree in organizational development. "Really, what you need is just a compassion and a concern for other people." She also says that because the field is an emerging one, you can go work for a firm that specializes in it, but "you really don't need to do that. You can kind of create your own expertise and market that."

"Don't allow yourself to be pressured by other peoples' expectations of you, and if there's something that you really want to do, go for it." If you are confused about deciding what you want to do, be true to that. "Don't be afraid to make mistakes, have successes and failures." Sujata says that you don't have to fit into a rigid mold. "You can't be a good mother, you can't be a good wife, you can't be a good daughter if you don't like what you're doing."

Helpful Personality Traits

Compassionate, approachable, exceptional listener, willing to be a facilitator, able to let go of work, and an interest in human beings and their well-being.

Hobbies & Interests

Travel, cooking, desire to make documentary films, hanging out with friends and family, reading, and researching personal-growth issues.

> A *focus group* is a group of people selected to discuss insights, ideas, opinions, and observations about a certain topic or product.

Susan Dickerson

Staff Anesthesiologist

{ *"You can go in and take someone who would otherwise wake up in agonizing pain... and they wake up almost pain free, resting comfortably."* }

Job Description

Susan oversees the anesthetic care of people in three to four operating rooms that are centrally located within a large suite of a hospital. While a *nurse anesthetist* administers the *anesthesia* to a patient, Susan is there for its induction and when the patient "wakes up." She remains accessible to the nurse anesthetists at all times by cell phone, but will perform other anesthetic procedures as needed. "I may run up to OB [obstetrics] to do a labor *epidural*. I may be called to do an *intubation* in the emergency department or for cardiac arrest somewhere in the hospital."

A Day on the Job

Performs pre-operational interviews with patients. • Checks on operating rooms hourly to see how her patients are doing. • Supervises patients' care as they awake from surgery. • Performs anesthetic procedures when necessary. • Performs pain clinics. "We are consulted by a primary-care person... typically a neurosurgeon or orthopedist, to do specialized injections when not supervising in the operating room."

Job Likes

"I really enjoy being part of the real big team that we are… supporting the surgeons and supporting the nurses." • "I like doing patient care. I like talking to people; they're interesting." • "I have to have hand-eye skills. It's procedure-oriented, and I enjoy that." • Susan really likes that she gives people pain relief from surgical procedures. "You can go in and take someone who would otherwise wake up in agonizing pain… and they wake up almost pain free, resting comfortably."

Job Challenges

The medical field can be stressful because of what insurance will and won't pay for. Susan says, "There's always less money, and there's always more work, and that stretches you thin." • "Every now and then you'll work with a team member who has a personality disorder… and they can make your life fairly miserable."

Steps to Current Job

- Presbyterian College, Clinton, South Carolina; Bachelor of Science in Chemistry.
- Medical University of South Carolina, Charleston; Medical Doctor (M.D.).
- Obstetrics internship with the U.S. Navy for one year.
- General-practice internship with the U.S. Navy for two years.
- Naval Hospital in San Diego, California; residency in Anesthesiology for three years.
- Anesthesiologist.

Advice

Susan laughs remembering her entrance into the medical profession. She said, "I would not do it the way that I did it. I think that it would be better to make the decision [to be an anesthesiologist] with knowledge ahead of time of what you are really getting into. I would say spend time working in a hospital. I knew nothing. Get a job as a lab tech, EMT [emergency medical technician], or hospital volunteer, so you get some exposure to medicine.

Remember that you need to take care of yourself before you even think about getting married and having a family. Susan says, "Plan your life around you taking the responsibility for getting where you want to go and getting what you want. Do not hang all of your hopes on a guy, and your first priority needs to be your friends and family—your support system."

Helpful Personality Traits

Enjoy biology and have a backbone of steel: "I'm fairly type-A [driven] and forceful… and surgeons are also that type of personality, and they will run you over in a heartbeat. You've got to be able to handle people yelling at you and cursing at you because that happens. It's an intense field and intense stuff happens... dealing with life-and-death decisions."

Hobbies & Interests

Gardening, singing sacred and other choral music, reading novels and 18th century literature, aerobics, clogging, and teaching Sunday school.

Anesthesia is the process of blocking the perception of pain and other sensations. This allows patients to undergo surgery and other procedures without the distress and pain they would otherwise experience. There are several forms of anesthesia:

- General anesthesia—with reversible loss of consciousness.

- Local anesthesia—with reversible loss of sensation in a (small) part of the body by localized administration of anesthetic drugs at the affected site.

- Regional anesthesia—with reversible loss of sensation and possibly movement in a region of the body by selective blockade of sections of the spinal cord or nerves supplying the region.[1]

An *epidural* is regional anesthesia resulting from injection of an anesthetic into the epidural space of the spinal cord; sensation is lost in the abdominal and genital and pelvic areas; used in childbirth and gynecological surgery.[2]

A *nurse anesthetist* is a nurse practitioner who has achieved through master-level classes certification to administer anesthesia.

Intubation is the placement of a tube into an external or internal orifice of the body.[3]

---

[1] http://en.wikipedia.org/wiki/Anesthesia

[2] www.websters-online-dictionary.org/definition/english/Ep/Epidural.html

[3] http://en.wikipedia.org/wiki/Intubation

Terri Gruca

Weekend News Anchor and Consumer Reporter

{ *"You're gonna work weekends, you're gonna work odd hours, and you're gonna work holidays because the news does not stop."* }

Job Description

On Saturdays and Sundays, Terri is a news anchor for a television station. She gathers current news from news crews and her own sources, writes a short synopsis about each news story, and then presents these stories in a televised newscast. When she's not anchoring the news, Terri works as a consumer reporter, where she collects information about a specific topic and records a presentation of her findings to be aired during a newscast. "I'll do everything from testing a product to see if it works, to investigations on companies that may have wronged people in the public... pretty much anything that deals with money."

A Day on the Job

Weekend News Anchor

Meets with the show's producers to talk about the day's events. • Checks e-mail and phone messages. • Writes a 15- to 20-second synopsis about area and national news stories. This might involve looking through videotape footage shot by the news crews. • Prepares for the show about 30 minutes before it airs (Terri does her own hair and makeup). • Arrives on the set about 10 minutes before the show starts. "I've already read through what I am going to read on the air that night." • Presents a 30-minute newscast. • Reads through the next show. • Back on the set for the next 30-minute newscast. Terri anchors three evening newscasts on Saturday and two on Sunday.

Consumer Reporter

Checks e-mails and phone messages. • Attends a 9 a.m. meeting where everyone from the news department talks about the last show and what is going on that day. Ideas for consumer reports are "pitched" in this meeting. • Returns e-mail and phone messages. • Goes out on shoots. "I schedule my shoots usually two weeks in advance. I have the product already and then I've researched it. So I have an idea of some of the things I'm looking to test." • Returns to the station to watch the videotape footage. • Writes the story. • Records her presentation.

Job Likes

This job combines Terri's love of writing and her joy in meeting new people. • "I think it's just a great way to not only know a little bit about what's happening before anybody else does, but to share it with people." • "The great thing about my job is that I feel that I am constantly learning something new." • "I've gotten to travel quite a bit. I've gotten to go to places that I would have never probably gone to had I not been doing this as a career." • "It's not a desk job. I think for people who can't see themselves sitting behind a desk everyday, this is a great career to consider."

Job Challenges

"You're gonna work weekends, you're gonna work odd hours, and you're gonna work holidays because the news does not stop. I've been in this business 10 years and I will work this Christmas." • Terri's career has required her to move often, and she sometimes finds it tough to be so far away from family. The flip side to this is that Terri finds it exciting to meet new people and become a part of new communities. • "Our careers can be pretty demanding," which makes it difficult to plan a life outside of work.

Steps to Current Job

- The University of North Carolina at Chapel Hill, Bachelor of Arts in Journalism. Worked as a Chyron operator (typed the text seen on newscasts) for a local news channel during her last two years of school.
- Reporter and photographer for three and a half years.
- Anchor for morning and noon newscasts for three years.
- Solo anchor, primary fill-in anchor and daily consumer/investigative reporter for two years.
- Weekend anchor and consumer reporter for one and a half years.

Advice

"I would say learn as much as you can about writing. Also, take advantage of any internships you possibly can because that's where you're going to get the most practical experience, and I think the best feel for what really is involved in the job, day in and day out."

"Don't be afraid to follow your heart. Nowadays we're so fortunate that we have so many opportunities and possibilities of doing exactly what it is we want to do. Don't let anybody tell you, 'You can't do it,' regardless of what it is." Terri had some people along the way that told her television is difficult to break into, and that not many people can make it. She didn't listen to them and look where she's landed. Terri also believes that "women can have it all nowadays. I think we just have to make decisions as to when we have it all."

Helpful Personality Traits

Curious, good writer, people person, and a good communicator in a genuine way.

Hobbies & Interests

Reading, working out, scrapbooking, travel, and spending time with family.

Theresa Wagoner

Physical Therapist

{ *"I love anatomy and science."* }

Job Description

Theresa works as a physical therapist for a wellness center. The majority of her clients have sports-related injuries, and she helps them recover, maintain, and improve their level of strength and mobility through education, strengthening exercises, and manual therapy. Physical therapists work with a variety of patient-care challenges, including accident victims, post-surgery patients, burn victims, cerebral palsy patients, patients with back pain, geriatric patients, and so on.

A Day on the Job

Sees two to three patients a day. Theresa's schedule is light because she works part-time while raising her young children. • Interviews the patient to gain an understanding of his or her problem. She asks questions such as these: When did the injury happen? What were you doing? What goal do you want to achieve through therapy? • Assesses the patient's overall physical condition and the area of injury. • Educates the patient about his or her injury, explaining why it occurred and how to keep it from happening again. • Stretches and instructs her patient with gym equipment to strengthen the injured area—Theresa emphasizes, "only when appropriate and when acute pain subsides." • Performs manual therapy to the injured area. This is somewhat like a massage, but Theresa works with the tissue around the area of injury. "Basically it's my hands doing something to their soft tissue or to their joints." • May use heat or ice to treat the area of attention. Many physical therapists also use ultrasound and electrical stimulation.

Job Likes

"I like the flexibility." Theresa is an avid athlete. She sets her work schedule around her own personal workout schedule and her children's schedules. • "I like helping people help themselves." • "I love anatomy and science."

Job Challenges

"Having to ask people to pay for it." Many people at the wellness center think that physical therapy is included in their membership, and it causes confusion when Theresa asks them to pay. • When Theresa worked in an outpatient clinic, she did not enjoy dealing with insurance companies. "Trying to convince somebody that doesn't know anything about the patient I'm working with, why what I was doing was necessary," was something she disliked.

Steps to Current Job

- Ithaca College in New York; Bachelor of Science in Physical Therapy.
- Physical therapist for various hospitals and outpatient clinics for five years.
- Assistant director of an outpatient clinic for one and a half years.
- Took time off to spend time with her young child for five years.
- Part-time physical therapist.

Advice

Theresa received her bachelor's degree in physical therapy before a master's was required to practice. Today, you must have a master's in physical therapy in order to be licensed. While you are in PT school, you will be exposed to all areas of physical therapy. Theresa advises not to pick your specialty until you've completed the program. After graduation and fulfilling a required amount of work hours, you have the option to become more specialized in areas such as sports medicine, pediatrics, geriatrics, neurology, and so on. (See the American Physical Therapy Association Web site at www.apta.org for more information.)

"Don't do something because you think that's what other people want you to. It's hard to get up in the morning" to go to a job that you don't like. You should follow what it is you want to do because "In 10 years, you're the one going to work everyday," not the person who thought that career was good for you.

Helpful Personality Traits

Patient, enjoys teaching, and persevering.

Hobbies & Interests

Exercising (running races), outdoor activities, reading, and travel.

Tonya Baker

Pharmacist

{ *"Anywhere you go, there's a job."* }

Job Description
Tonya is a registered pharmacist and works for a chain drugstore. She is responsible for the distribution of prescription drugs to the public.

A Day on the Job
Works three 10-hour shifts each week. This is considered a full-time pharmacist position in her company. • Takes prescription orders from physicians' offices. • Enters data into the computer. • Communicates with insurance companies about patient accounts. • Fills prescriptions. • Counsels customers: "How to take the medication. What side-effects to look for. What adverse reactions may happen… basically what to expect after you start taking the medication." She also gives over-the-counter drug suggestions. • Advises doctors on pharmaceutical questions. • Supervises pharmacy technicians. "That's the biggest part of the day," and it reminds Tonya that being a pharmacy technician with the national certification program is also another route if pharmacology interests you. • Performs quality-assurance checks. "The last person to see it [the filled prescription] is a pharmacist."

Job Likes
"I like working with the public… giving my knowledge as best I can." • "I like being busy, feeling like I'm needed throughout the day and not just sitting there waiting for something to happen. There is always something to do." • "I have days off during the week, as well as at least every other weekend in most situations." • "Anywhere you go, there's a job."

Job Challenges
"Probably just the long hours."

Steps to Current Job

- Took college courses during high school at Chattanooga State Technical Community College in Tennessee.
- The University of Tennessee at Chattanooga for three years. Tonya continued to take some courses at Chattanooga State Technical Community College to save money.
- Samford University in Birmingham, Alabama, McWhorter School of Pharmacy; completed a four-year Pharmacy Doctorate (Pharm.D.) program. Interned with CVS and Wal-Mart while in school.
- Started working for one of the pharmacy chains where she interned.

Advice

"I think it's a great career for women. Mainly because you work three to four days of the week. If you want to become a mom and be a stay-at-home, part-time employee, then you can still make a very decent salary." Tonya points out are that most chain pharmacies offer great benefits. As far as school is concerned, Tonya stresses not to let the length of time that pharmacy school requires intimidate you. She also thinks that "it's not necessarily hard information to learn; there's just a lot of it. So don't think that you're not smart enough to be there." Tonya says that there is a lot of variety within pharmacy. Besides retail, there are also opportunities in hospital, nuclear, research, and clinical pharmacy and with pharmaceutical companies.

"There's no limit. You can do whatever you want. It's not a man-driven world anymore. As far as pharmacy is concerned, two-thirds of the pharmacy students are women now."

Helpful Personality Traits

Good communicator, confident, outgoing, compassionate, patient, and responsible.

Hobbies & Interests

Crafts, sewing, puzzles, games, hiking, travel, and yard work.

"The more passions and desires one has, the more ways one has of being happy."

—Catherine-Charlotte de Gramont,
17th-Century Princess of Monaco

Tracy Church

Director of Development (Fund-Raising) for The Johns Hopkins Heart Institute, Part of The Fund for Johns Hopkins Medicine

{ *"Often it is uncertain from where the funding for innovative, untested ideas will come; yet these ideas contain the seeds for future treatments and cures."* }

Job Description
Tracy raises money that supports research, education, and patient care for cardio-vascular services (cardiology and cardiac surgery).

A Day on the Job
Contacts prospective financial donors and lets them know what Johns Hopkins is doing to prevent, diagnose, treat, and cure heart disease. • Meets with physicians and donors or potential donors. • Travels to visit donors and potential donors. • Follows up on visits with donors and potential donors with letters, phone calls, meetings, proposals for philanthropic commitments, campus tours, and event invitations. Tracy also writes reports about the visit and enters donor information in a database. • Creates broad strategies to build The Heart Institute's development programs over longer periods of time. • Writes letters, proposals, reports, and other documents. • Researches possible donors. • Reads newspapers, such as the *New York Times, Washington Post, Wall Street Journal,* and *Baltimore Sun.*

Job Likes
"It is very satisfying to participate in the process of getting people excited about the mission of Hopkins Medicine." • "I really enjoy learning about the human body and the complex systems that govern it." Tracy then takes this knowledge and explains it in a way that the average person can understand and see its importance.

Job Challenges
Because medical research is so expensive, Tracy is sometimes "overwhelmed at the amount needed to accomplish Hopkins' goals."

Steps to Current Job
- University of Florida, Gainesville, Bachelor of Science in Accounting and Finance.
- Certified Public Accountant (CPA) for six years.
- Director of development and donor relations for the University of North Carolina Medical School for three years.
- Assistant Director of Development at the University of Maryland for one year.
- Tracy has worked at The Johns Hopkins Heart Institute since 2001, where she has held the following positions:
  - Assistant director of development for one year.
  - Associate director of development for three years.
  - Director of development.

Advice
If you're interested in development for an educational institution, Tracy suggests that you get involved in public-speaking activities, such as the debate team and school or community plays. If an opportunity for fund-raising at school or in the community arises, get involved. Tracy also thinks that volunteering for a local organization that supports your interests is a great way to try activities and build skills.

Really think about how you like to spend your day. As a CPA, Tracy found that the majority of her time was spent analyzing data. Today, she spends most of her time dealing with people and is a lot happier.

Tracy also says to enjoy your education and to pursue any subject that interests you. Spending time with people who share those interests is a great way to learn more. In the end, she says, "life is very short. Take risks and challenge yourself."

Helpful Personality Traits
Good listener, considerate, enjoy working with people and respect their accomplishments, bold, tenacious, thinks big, and persistent.

Hobbies & Interests
Hanging out and getting to know people, ballet (she performs with a local ballet company), gardening, reading, and shopping.

> *Johns Hopkins Medicine* is the medical school and learning hospital affiliated with Johns Hopkins University.

Wanda Revis

Community College Instructor

{ *"I love the interaction with the students because it's so exciting to see a student grow and change."* }

Job Description
Wanda is a nursing instructor at a community college. "I teach nursing students the skills and behaviors they need to provide patient care."

A Day on the Job
Lectures classes. Wanda teaches fundamentals of nursing, patient-care skills, clinical-care skills, and management and leadership. • Leads an on-campus laboratory where students practice skills learned in lectures. • Oversees students at local health-care facilities where they apply the skills learned in class and in the laboratory. • Develops curriculum and program content, which includes evaluating textbooks, updating course materials, and serving on campus committees. • Keeps office hours to make herself available to students.

Job Likes
"I love the interaction with the students because it's so exciting to see a student grow and change. The faculty that are involved in this program are here because they truly want to help others succeed in becoming a nurse." • "I love the interaction with the patients. I am not now practicing as a nurse in a traditional setting, but to be able to go into the facilities each week and interact with patients… is a really rewarding experience." • "I like that my job is flexible."

Job Challenges
Wanda had a hard time thinking of job dislikes. However, "we are challenged as faculty to make the course interesting, innovative, and fun for the student."

Steps to Current Job
- Clemson University in Clemson, South Carolina; Bachelor of Science in Nursing.
- Arizona State University in Tempe; Master of Science in Nursing (MSN).

- Health-care management for a home-health agency for 13 years.
- Instructor for a community college.

Advice

Wanda advises readers to get as much education and experience as you can. Experience allows you to be a better teacher and gives you credibility. "The reason I would say more education is because the more that you have, the more choices you have for environments to work in, and you'll always be able to go anywhere and teach. You definitely need a master's degree in order to teach at the community college level. You need a Ph.D. in order to be tenured as a professor at the four-year, B.S. [bachelor of science] level."

"The fact is there are no boundaries now for women, and we can be anything, go anywhere, do anything we want to do. It's a very exciting time, I think, to be a young woman. The only limitations you have are the ones you place on yourself. The possibilities and opportunities are there for you to be whatever you want to be."

Helpful Personality Traits

Intelligent, compassionate, enjoy interacting with others, good communication skills, and excitement and enthusiasm for helping others.

Hobbies & Interests

Singing, hiking, and reading.

Whitney Corrigan

Pediatric Oncology Nurse

{ *"It is such an honor to be allowed into their lives."* }

Job Description

Whitney is a registered nurse at a federally funded research hospital in the pediatric *oncology*, *hematology*, and *immunology* unit. Whitney takes care of her patients' daily needs by giving medications and monitoring their health condition. She works with pediatric and young-adult patients who have cancer, HIV, and inherited immune problems.

A Day on the Job

Listens to an audio report recorded by a nurse from the previous shift. The tape gives Whitney an update about each patient. She takes care of one to four patients per day, depending on how sick they are. • Assesses patients by taking vital signs, asking what they need, and preparing them for the day's events. • Gives medications intravenously (IV) or orally. Medicines can include antibiotics, pain medication, and chemotherapy. • All of Whitney's patients are volunteering for medical research. This requires extra monitoring specific to each research study • Educates patients about their illnesses and the medications or other interventions they are receiving. • Monitors patients for sudden changes in condition. • Works closely with the patients' doctors, especially when she or the doctor has concerns about a patient. "I work very closely with the doctors, and I make sure that they are aware of what's going on with the patient." • Ensures the quality of life for terminally ill patients and their families, making sure they are comfortable while at the hospital. "The focus of the care is different. Our focus on taking care of them changes from fixing the problem… to making sure that they are comfortable and getting the quality of life that they deserve up until the end." • Documents everything that happens that day and enters it into the computer. • Tape-records patient updates for the following shift.

Job Likes

Whitney recalls this quote from nursing school: "Nursing is an honor because you are with people at the most intimate times of their lives." She expands upon this to say that she is with her patients during very difficult times and feels "it is such an honor to be allowed into their lives." • "I really like the people that I work with. I think that people who work in the field of pediatric oncology, and pediatrics in general, have a good outlook on life and have a good perspective. I think the job that we've got teaches us to appreciate the life that we've got." • "I also enjoy getting to know families and helping them in a time that is really important to them." • "I was considering going into medical school. One of the reasons I chose nursing was because I knew it would give me flexibility when I had a family." Whitney went part-time when she had her first child. She says that now her full-time job is being a mother, and her part-time job is being a nurse.

Job Challenges

"A hospital has to be open 24 hours a day, seven days a week, holidays, weekends, all through the night. Working the holidays is probably the thing I like the least."

Steps to Current Job

- University of North Carolina at Chapel Hill, Bachelor of Arts in Psychology and Bachelor of Science in Nursing.

- Cancer nursing internship for nine months with a cancer research institute.
- Registered nurse with a federally funded research hospital.

Advice

Nursing school can be stressful and requires a lot of "busywork." Whitney says to remember that the job is not as bad as the schooling! She also advises, "don't limit yourself to one idea of what nursing is because there are so many amazing jobs for nurses now." Other nursing avenues Whitney mentions are research, acquiring a more advanced degree, and sales in pharmaceuticals or medical products.

Helpful Personality Traits

Compassionate and an aptitude for and enjoyment of science and math.

Hobbies & Interests

Spending time with her husband and children and cross-stitching.

Oncology is the study of cancer or tumors.

Hematology is the study of blood.

Immunology is the study of the immune system.

Epilogue

Firestarters is just a sampling of the many career opportunities available to you. If you find something that "sparks" your interest, learn more about it. Search the Internet; go to the library; volunteer in that field; and talk with your parents, teachers, and friends. Even if none of these jobs appeals to you, we hope that you've learned some tools and are inspired to try to find a career that is right for you.

So often, we are defined by what we do. Whatever it is that you choose, be proud of it. Be yourself. Be positive. Enjoy life. And remember, you are in control of your destiny. What fire is burning in you?

"Each of us has a fire in our hearts for something. It's our goal in life to find it and keep it lit."

—Mary Lou Retton

Index